7³

When I Grow Up...

I Want To Be An Adult

BY **Ron Ross**

Christ-Centered Recovery Workbook for Adult Children

Recovery Publications, Inc.
1201 Knoxville Street
San Diego, CA 92110
(619) 275-1350

D1360048

Published by
Recovery Publications, Inc.
1201 Knoxville Street
San Diego, CA 92110-3718
(619) 275-1350

Scripture quotations marked (NIV) are from the *Holy Bible, New International Version* and are used with permission. Copyright © 1973, 1978, 1984 by International Bible Society.

Scripture quotations marked (KJV) are from the *Holy Bible, King James Version*, by Thomas Nelson Inc., Publishers.

The Twelve Steps are reprinted and adapted with permission of Alcoholics Anonymous World Services, Inc. Permission to reprint and adapt the Twelve Steps does not mean that AA has reviewed or approved the content of this publication, nor that AA agrees with the views expressed herein. AA is a program of recovery from alcoholism. Use of the Twelve Steps in connection with programs and activities which are patterned after AA but which address other problems does not imply otherwise.

The material from *The Twelve Steps—A Spiritual Journey* has been reprinted and adapted with permission. Copyright © 1988 by Recovery Publications, Inc.

NOTICE:

This book is designed to provide information regarding the subject matter covered. It is provided with the understanding that the publisher and author are not engaged in rendering professional services.

Printed in the United States of America

Library of Congress Catalog Card No. 90-60660

Second Printing April 1991

Recovery Publications, Inc.
Distributed by The Fleming H. Revell Company

    When I Grow Up . . . I Want To Be An Adult: Christ-Centered Recovery Workbook for Adult Children

ISBN: 0-941405-15-X

Dedication

Without the loving cooperation of
my beloved wife and children,
my recovery in Christ
would be less than...

Without the guidance of Brother Mickey,
I might have short circuited
Christ's best.

I dedicate this work to them.

Thanks!

Table of Contents

The Twelve Steps of Alcoholics Anonymous

1. We admitted we were powerless over alcohol—that our lives had become unmanageable. 2. Came to believe that a Power greater than ourselves could restore us to sanity. 3. Made a decision to turn our will and our lives over to the care of God as we understood Him. 4. Made a searching and fearless moral inventory of ourselves. 5. Admitted to God, to ourselves, and to another human being the exact nature of our wrongs. 6. Were entirely ready to have God remove all these defects of character. 7. Humbly asked Him to remove our shortcomings. 8. Made a list of all persons we had harmed, and became willing to make amends to them all. 9. Made direct amends to such people wherever possible, except when to do so would injure them or others. 10. Continued to take personal inventory and when we were wrong promptly admitted it. 11. Sought through prayer and meditation to improve our conscious contact with God as we understood Him, praying only for knowledge of His will for us and the power to carry that out. 12. Having had a spiritual awakening as the result of these steps, we tried to carry this message to alcoholics, and to practice these principles in all our affairs.

Foreword

. . . .

*T*oday, many adult Christians who were raised in dysfunctional families suffer from chronic emotional pain—pain brought on by years of parental torment and abuse. To some, the pain is undeniable because the abuse is so great. To others, the pain seems harmless because it is masked by a cavalier attitude.

The reality of being raised in this environment must be faced for life to proceed in a healthy way. Unresolved pain blocks serenity, spirituality and progress. All of us raised in an addictive or dysfunctional family were affected by this painful upbringing. Many of us developed coping skills to weather this often emotional storm—skills which now are outdated and need to be updated.

This book is about joining others in Christ-centered recovery and employing the power of group dynamics to heal our wounds. It is a helpful tool for Christians exploring recovery—be it their own recovery or that of a friend.

My own dysfunctional lifestyle was reordered by Jesus Christ. When I was at my darkest point, I asked him for help and received it in ways I never imagined. One of the vehicles he used to move me toward a fulfilling life was the intervention of other Christ-centered people. I now know that the most effective way to stay in recovery from addictions or compulsive behaviors is to join others in Christ in group settings to share our experience, strength and hope.

A loving and forgiving God saved me; how inspiring to read that God blessed Ron Ross in the same manner! I respect any method of treatment that works for people, but it is especially gratifying to find someone who shares my love of Christ and knows the difference he can make in one's healing and recovery.

When I Grow Up...**I Want To Be An Adult** is about Ron Ross' own personal tragedy and triumph over childhood abuse. More than that, it is a book that shares his story and offers a way to achieve similar triumphs. The material he presents is excellent for adult children wanting to find healing using these suggestions within the loving embrace of a Christ-centered recovery group.

Ron Ross exhibits deep faith through this work. He quotes Bible passages relevant to the issues he presents and shares practical suggestions and guidelines for recovering Christians. The end of each chapter contains individual and group questions for personal journaling and group discussion, as well as a suggested recovery tool to further aid the reader. In addition, guidelines for conducting Christ-centered recovery group sessions are presented.

This workbook is something we all need. Many times, when working with others in recovery, we have to be careful about expressing our Christian faith without offending someone. It is empowering to have a book specifically written to enable Christians to make the most of their faith in the recovery process.

My recovery process was empowered by my reaching out to help a young woman when I was in my own despair. She was one of the people Christ used to show me the way. This book is about more of the ways in which people can reach out to others in recovery. It shows how we can help those in our midst who are hurting and become disciples and healers in the way that Jesus taught us.

Jesus said, "*I tell you the truth, anyone who has faith in me will do what I have been doing. He will do even greater things than these because I am going to the Father.*" JOHN 14:12 (NIV). This message from Jesus proves that we can do things as great as he; that is why I see Christ-centered recovery groups as a powerful way to live out this Gospel message.

As an ordained minister, Ron's courage in sharing his own past lights the way for others to do the same. All of us in Christ's body, ordained and lay alike, benefit from shining the light on our darker sides. It is only then that we can begin to heal. I admire Ron Ross; he is a living example of accepting Christ's forgiveness to free himself to serve others in the Lord's name.

Sandra Simpson LeSourd
Author, *The Compulsive Woman*

Preface

. . . .

I was raised in a household of alcoholism, violence and abuse. As a result, my growth was stunted and I became one of the millions of "adult children" in our society today. Being raised in a home where there was severe deprivation and abuse caused me to develop chronologically but not emotionally.

When I reached adulthood, I was an emotional child trapped in an adult body. Too often, I related poorly to those around me and perpetuated the same behaviors which had damaged me so severely as a child. I am currently in recovery from this condition, and I attribute this to the intervention of Christ and Christ-centered people in my life.

This book is intended to help adult children recover from the traumas of their past. It is designed to offer ways to "grow up and become an adult" within the loving embrace of a Christ-centered recovery group. These suggestions are the result of my own searching as well as the experiences of people I have learned from and who supported me.

Twelve-step recovery groups such as Alcoholics Anonymous and Adult Children of Alcoholics have been highly successful in supporting people as they recover from their addictions. Such groups focus on the concept of a Higher Power as a vital part of their recovery. In this book, we learn to focus on Christ and his teachings as a vital part of our recovery.

If a living organism gets stuck at any level of development, stagnation and degeneration can set in. Life demands growth, and the violation of that God-given principle causes severe and painful consequences. My personal growth was affected, and my life was stuck in pain, woundedness, life-destroying habits, bad relationships and sin. Admitting this was very difficult for me.

The narrative discusses facing up to "stuckness" and being exhorted, provoked and encouraged to move on to a brand new state of being—wholeness in Christ. In my life, Jesus represents harmonious, integrated, fulfilling, real and healthy living. He wants to infuse and impregnate our stagnate state of being with his wonderful life! This book is written to help the reader realize this and develop the ability to "grow up and be an adult."

No matter how damaged we have been, we all have the choice of opening ourselves to God's love and healing power through the Holy Spirit. *"Yet to all who received him, to those who believed in his name, he gave the right to become children of God."* JOHN 1:12 (NIV). When we invite Christ into our lives, the Holy Spirit can move into us and release new vitality in us. God does not violate us, invade us, force himself upon us or overtake us. When we open up to him, the Holy Spirit comes in and gently affirms us, reassuring us that God can be trusted.

To turn away from being stuck is to take the first step toward wholeness—to start moving forward. We can defy that sticky web of paralysis and degeneration by asking God to help us begin. When we ask the Holy Spirit to infuse us with the strength to take those first steps, we can move into wholeness! Most of us want to be mature adults when we grow up. Let us join together with Christ and begin our journey toward wholeness—toward becoming an adult!

Introduction

. . . .

*W*e live in a world of high-tech mass media and communication, linked together by telecommunication satellites, speed-of-sound transportation and fax machines. As a result, the pain of the whole world can become a part of our reality very quickly.

In a span of thirty minutes, we can be impacted by the horror of terrorist activity in the Middle East, kidnappings in Beirut, Third World freedom fighters, those struggling for democracy worldwide, the Columbian drug cartels—on and on it goes—hitting us squarely in the face, day in and day out. Meanwhile, we live with our own personal struggles.

I often feel sympathy for the families of hostages around the world, the blacks' struggle in South Africa, the homeless families everywhere, the single mother of five, the child being abused by an alcoholic father, as well as the fragile state of the world's peace and economy. I also share in the painful struggles of those I live and work with—the victims of abuse and deprivation in their childhood.

Within this world of suffering, there is hope for those who seek it. Christ-centered and secular self-help recovery communities are helping many people achieve wholeness and maturity by changing their behavior. In this book, recovery communities are defined as systems of support,

encouragement, personal identity and accountability among persons who meet together on a regular basis. The healing process seems to be most successful when people meet regularly in groups to share their experience, strength and hope in their recovery.

Self-help recovery communities are defined as support groups based on twelve-step programs such as Alcoholics Anonymous, Narcotics Anonymous, Al-Anon, Alateen, Adult Children of Alcoholics and a host of others. Such groups refer to God as a Higher Power, enabling people of diverse faiths to participate and benefit from their belief in God as they understand God. Members learn to draw upon their inner strength, to support each other and to affirm their belief in their Higher Power.

Christ-centered communities of recovery are similar in many ways to secular self-help recovery groups. Their main distinction is that the Christ-centered groups focus on the strength of a personal relationship with Jesus Christ as their Higher Power. In this way, the entire group becomes a living part of Christ's family.

Both Christ-centered and secular self-help groups create a safe and nurturing environment for their members. People feel safe, supported and affirmed as they deal with the pain in their lives. Participants do not escape the reality of their personal anguish or the world's pain; they face it and learn to deal with it effectively.

A vast network of secular self-help recovery fellowships has been developing over the past fifty years. I am in awe of their results and the scope of their reach. Twelve-step groups can be found in virtually every city in America and in many other countries. The network is grassroots, simple—and it works. People recover and get better in these fellowships and create a bond among themselves that is lasting.

In contrast, many churches have lost sight of the need to provide help to people who are hurting. They appear to be more concerned about well people than they are about hurting people. They fail to realize the potential for recovery within the church and often ignore the principal ministry of Jesus, which was to heal the wounded. Due to lack of support and knowledge within many churches, they sometimes turn from their responsibility and refer sick, hurting people and their families to secular self-help recovery groups.

As the reality of the world's ordeals continues to invade the churches, changes are being made. Pain and suffering among members is causing churches to become more aware of their obligation and opportunity to minister to the sick. Christ-centered fellowships are finally beginning to answer the call to be vehicles for healing and recovery.

There are not nearly enough Christ-centered recovery communities to meet the need, and many do not have the years of experience that the self-help groups do. This book is intended to help Christ-centered recovery communities become more supportive and work more effectively with people in pain. We do not yet have as clearly defined and as simple a structure as the secular self-help network, but we are headed in that direction. Literature about Christ-centered recovery resources is still very limited, but as we continue to gain experience and grow, more high-quality materials are becoming available.

My major focus is on Christ-centered communities of recovery for adult children, for it is here that I found my own healing. My work continues today in these communities, especially those dealing with young people who come from dysfunctional homes. My specific recovery community is Open Homes Ministries, P.O. Box 679022, Orlando, FL, 32867-9022; phone (407) 671-0900. Please feel free to contact us for resources and referrals for recovery programs.

I hope all of you who choose Christ-centered recovery will have the most rewarding experience possible. I firmly believe that all of us want to "grow up and become adults."

God Bless You!

How to Benefit Most from This Book

. . . .

*T*he purpose of this book is to introduce material which demonstrates the transforming power of Christ-centered recovery. It describes a step-by-step approach to discovering how we can share all of who we are—even the self-defeating thoughts and feelings we hide from ourselves and others. Through sharing honestly and openly with trusted friends, we begin to experience Christ's unconditional love for us through other people. We discover that being loved and cared for by those around us can help to transform our lives. We see that change is possible, and is a life-long process which involves focusing on God, ourselves and others.

This book is designed for use by individuals as well as groups. However the material is utilized, there are some basic guidelines to follow. Read the entire chapter before attempting to answer the questions at the end of the chapter. This provides an overall scope of the material being presented. The *Individual* and *Group Exercises* are important and help make the information in each chapter relevant.

Become familiar with the *Recovery Tool* at the end of each chapter and incorporate it into your ongoing work. Before using the tools, seriously consider creating a personal recovery journal. This is an effective way of recording your progress as you use each of the *Recovery Tools*. The journal can be a spiral-bound notebook, a three-ring binder with paper and dividers for each chapter, or a bound book with blank pages. The *Recovery Tool* at the end of the first chapter gives more details about a personal recovery journal.

Pace yourself through each chapter and allow sufficient time to complete the related questions. This may take a day or longer. Be patient with yourself; allow ample time to digest the content of each chapter and reflect on it meaning. Lack of patience can seriously impair your effectiveness.

The appendixes give complete guidelines for using this material in groups. Each meeting lasts two hours, starting and ending promptly. Experience in various meetings shows that trust develops most quickly in small "family groups" with a maximum of seven people. For example, if 24 people participate each week, it is recommended that this larger group be divided into four family groups with six members each. The family groups gather to complete the writing exercise and to share together for one hour. The final portion of the meeting is devoted to sharing in one, all-inclusive group.

When participants surrender to guidance from the Holy Spirit, problems can be handled in a constructive and respectful manner. As adult children, we are inclined to be caretakers, enablers and people-pleasers as indicated by our inability to confront inappropriate, hurtful, or self-destructive behavior. Instead, we tend to be overly nice to others. In keeping with the need for a safe environment, excessive confrontation is not recommended. However, straightforward feedback is critically important, with communication being limited to each one's personal experience in a given situation.

Inappropriate behaviors and feelings may have dominated our lives and seem natural to us. As we progress through recovery, our tendency to view negative behavior as normal begins to change. We experience growth in all areas as our self-worth and self-esteem increase. We stop anticipating hurtful experiences and accept and appreciate our positive experiences. It is important to affirm and encourage one another's healthy feelings and behaviors as this change begins to take place.

Wherever possible, share your insights with someone you trust. Seek a special relationship with at least one other person in recovery—a fellow pilgrim who is trustworthy and committed to Christ-centered recovery. Intimate and confidential communication with another person can work miracles. Be aware that your listener is not there to give advice or to counsel you, unless trained and licensed to do so. Healing comes from your relationship with the Lord.

You may also wish to develop relationships with other participants in your support group. They can become a part of your extended family and a vital lifeline to ongoing recovery in Christ.

There is no right or wrong way to use the material in this book and no one is being graded on performance. Individuals experience the same material and the same group differently. People grow and change at their own rates and according to their own needs. Progress should be measured only be each participant monitoring his or her own successes.

This workbook offers readers various ideas and suggestions which may be adapted in different ways. The primary objective of the program is for those involved in it to gain the maximum value from their participation. It is important to become familiar with and understand the dynamics of this material. Be clear about what you are expected to do, and be aware of the function of the leaders and other group members. *Appendix Two* and *Appendix Three* introduce the structure and process of the program. All participants should review them before beginning the workbook material.

Appendix Two
- Guidelines for Forming and Leading a Study Group
- Suggested Meeting Announcement
- Suggested Meeting Schedule
- Suggested Family Group Roster

Appendix Three
- Suggested Study Group Meeting Format
  Introductory Meeting
  Week One Meeting
  Week Two Meeting
  Week Three to Week Ten Meeting

Invitation to Christ-Centered Recovery

. . . .

*I*f you are an adult child just beginning recovery, I have an idea how much you are hurting. Let's look at it together. Walk with me for a while on a journey toward wholeness. We may discover we lived in similar painful circumstances or grew up in similar homes. Even though we are strangers, we may have a lot in common through our shared history. From my experience alone, I sense we have all been exposed to many hurtful conditions. Pain has no cultural, racial, religious, socio-economic, intellectual, or doctrinal boundaries. It crosses every line.

I am in recovery, and I know how much it helps when someone else cares enough to share their own experience, strength and hope. It helps me to know others are with me. I spent many years alone in my agony, and I realize how important it is that we have each other. God made us to be his family and to live in community, loving and helping one another. Writing this book is my way of sharing how Christ helped me face the reality of the deep wounds I denied for so long and how he is currently guiding me in my recovery.

God has paved a pathway of recovery for all of us through Jesus' personal suffering on the cross. We have all received an open invitation to benefit from Jesus' walk on earth. He said, "...*Come to me, all you who are weary and burdened, and I will give you rest.*" MATTHEW 11:28 (NIV). There is great comfort in the arms of Christ, open to all who seek him.

The Bible describes Jesus as a great high priest, which I understand to simply mean that he has gone through every kind of human pain and suffering. Thus, Christ can identify with all of us. When I first began to comprehend that he truly understood what I was going through, I was astounded! "*For we do not have a high priest who is unable to sympathize with our weaknesses, but we have one who has been tempted in every way, just as we are—yet was without sin. Let us then approach the throne of grace with confidence, so that we may receive mercy and find grace to help us in our time of need.*" HEBREWS 4:15-16 (NIV). I chose to accept God's invitation to receive mercy and found grace through the work of the Holy Spirit.

Jesus has also been referred to as the great physician, and in the Bible he says "...*'It is not the healthy who need a doctor, but the sick.'*" MATTHEW 9:12 (NIV). I thought I needed a human doctor to cure me. Instead, I found what I really needed was the great physician—Christ. I knew I needed someone who could help me handle my pain, weariness, burdens and weaknesses— someone who wouldn't kick me when I was down—someone who had also been there. I didn't know where to find that person until Christ came into my life.

I tried playing doctor and pharmacist and medicating my pain with chemicals and food. Adding insult to injury, I found the help of professional counselors to be superficial and expensive. The assistance I received from secular self-help recovery groups only encouraged me to cope for a while longer—it didn't truly satisfy my needs. I came to see that any help I provided for myself was short-lived. At the end of my human resources, the idea of a great physician was very comforting to me. What good news it was to discover how Christ identifies with my pain, paves the way for my healing and then pays the bill!

Not only was the idea of a great high priest and a great physician unbelievable to me at first, I was sure that even if Christ was real, he wouldn't choose to help me. I had hurt a lot of others in response to my own suffering, and I didn't feel I deserved God's help. I envisioned myself as being beyond help—unworthy and too far gone. I was convinced that coping with my pain was the only thing I could do.

In my mind, healing, recovery and wholeness were unattainable dreams. Solomon pegged my condition perfectly when he wrote, "*Who has woe? Who has sorrow? Who has strife? Who has complaints? Who has needless bruises? Who has bloodshot eyes?...Your eyes will see strange sights and your mind imagine confusing things. You will be like one sleeping on the high seas, lying on top of the rigging. 'They hit me,' you will say, 'but I am not hurt! They beat me, but I don't feel it!...'*" PROVERBS 23:29,33-35 (NIV).

Before deciding whether or not to commit to Christ-centered recovery, you must accept that Jesus, the son of God, the great high priest and great physician, gave his life on the cross to offer us this help. Jesus is unlike anyone else we've ever known. "*...He had no beauty or majesty to attract us to him, nothing in his appearance that we should desire him. He was despised and rejected by men, a man of sorrows, and familiar with suffering. Like one from whom men hide their faces, he was despised and we esteemed him not. Surely he took up our infirmities and carried our sorrows...But he was pierced for our transgressions, he was crushed for our iniquities; the punishment that brought us peace was upon him, and by his wounds we are healed...and the Lord has laid on him the iniquity of us all. He was oppressed and afflicted, yet he did not open his mouth; he was led like a lamb to the slaughter, and as a sheep before her shearers is silent, so he did not open his mouth...for the transgression of my people he was stricken.*" ISAIAH 53:2-8 (NIV).

This same Jesus lives in me today and in countless others in Christ-centered recovery communities. He invites us to examine and apply his healing truths to our own lives. My desire is to present God to you right where you hurt. The Holy Spirit salves and heals my wounds, one by one, as I give him access to them. If you choose to give Christ access to your pain, to receive him as the great high priest and physician in your life, he will heal you, too. I invite you to join me in looking to the Holy Spirit for healing and recovery as you move through pain and sadness into wholeness and joy in a recovery community of your own choosing. As part of Christ-centered recovery, we can receive insight and courage through prayer, meditation and Bible study.

There are many illustrations from Scripture that can provide a foundation for recovery. The **Parable of the Good Samaritan** from Luke 10:30-35 (NIV) is one example:

"A man was going down from Jerusalem to Jericho, when he fell into the hands of robbers. They stripped him of his clothes, beat him and went away, leaving him half dead."

A child was living in a painful situation at the mercy of those who abused, deprived, manipulated, or otherwise afflicted him. He grew up stripped of dignity, self-respect and personal identity.

"A priest happened to be going down the same road, and when he saw the man, he passed by on the other side."

A religious person or secular professional saw this person when he grew older and got into trouble but refused to get involved.

"So too, a Levite, when he came to the place and saw him, passed by on the other side."

A legalist who thought the person probably deserved his condition passed judgment on him with self-righteous indignation.

"But a Samaritan, as he traveled, came where the man was; and when he saw him, he took pity on him."

A friend from a Christ-centered recovery community approached the person, having been in the same ditch himself only months before, and treated him with compassion coming from the strength of his own personal recovery.

"He went to him and bandaged his wounds, pouring on oil and wine."

The friend become personally involved and comforted the person with the healing ointment of Jesus, pouring on the gifts of the Holy Spirit who lived inside him.

"Then he put the man on his own donkey, took him to an inn and took care of him."

Then the friend told him about Christ-centered support groups, took him to a halfway house or treatment center and supported him in his recovery.

"The next day he took out two silver coins and gave them to the innkeeper."

The next day he made available some of the resources pooled in recovery groups for people who need help.

"Look after him,' he said, 'and when I return, I will reimburse you for any extra expense you may have.'"

The person received aftercare in a supportive atmosphere.

This is but one illustration of the principles upon which Christ-centered recovery is founded. Many individuals in recovery communities can readily testify to being rescued from a ditch alongside the road of life. I am still traveling on this same road to recovery, even as I share my personal story with you.

God does care about us; he does love us. It is up to you to choose to surrender yourself to this belief and experience the joys and wholeness of growing up and becoming an adult.

Chapter One

Who Am I?

. . . .

*O*h my God, Fred finally did what he promised—he killed Mother! Next he'll come after all of us—Donnie, Kenny, Debbie and me." Those were my first thoughts as I awakened to the piercing crack of what I knew was my stepfather's gun. He often threatened us with it. Was the shot part of a nightmare or was it real?

We each had our own bedroom in the house on Maryland Avenue. It was the fourth house we had lived in since Mom had been with Fred. I was eleven years old. Donnie and I were twins and the oldest in the family. Kenny was eighteen months younger and Debbie was six years younger than Donnie and I.

Our real Dad left us when Donnie and I were six, so as the oldest boys we became the defenders of the family. When Fred first came into our lives, we were not afraid; we wrote his threats off as the demands of a crazy drunk. It wasn't until we lived with him awhile and his abuse escalated that we became fearful of him. I knew Fred was unhappy, especially with us. The entire time I knew him, he seemed tense and angry around us.

Seconds after I heard the shot ring out in the early morning hours I thought, "He's coming. I hear his steps on the stairs. He shot Mom and is now coming to shoot each one of us."

Thoughts of Fred's craziness raced through my mind. The painful memories of being forbidden to eat until he had, prohibited from talking while he was at home, restricted from sitting on his furniture, banished to my room whenever I forgot to do a chore flooded my brain. The sounds of Fred's screaming rages; my mother's crying, pleading and yelling; Donnie and I cussing him as we tried to fight back and Debbie crying herself to sleep night after night reverberated in my head as I lay there trying to grasp what was happening.

For many years, I tried hard to please Fred. I even started signing his name as my last name. However, I soon realized that Fred didn't want me to use his last name, so I stopped. I felt I didn't belong anywhere. No matter how hard I tried, I never seemed to please him.

My heart raced as I listened intently in the silence. "Is Mom dead? Is Fred dead? Am I dreaming? Did I imagine the footsteps?" My mind would not stop.

At that moment, I realized that I was lying in a pool of my own urine. I was embarrassed that I still wet the bed at the age of eleven. Everyone in my family made fun of me. Fred often brought up my bed-wetting in public. I wouldn't spend the night with my only two friends because I was afraid of wetting the bed, and Donnie and Kenny hated to sleep in the same bed with me whenever we went to Grandma's. I even believed I could never get married because of my bed-wetting. It didn't seem to matter what I tried to do, it still happened. I was eighteen years old when I finally quit wetting the bed.

"Ronnie, open the door," I heard Mother whisper outside my bedroom door. So I really had heard footsteps, and they were Mom's! A moment of joy replaced the flood of fear as I realized she wasn't dead. I quickly opened my door, and Mother said, "Fred is passed out on the floor. He shot at me and missed." She told me to call the police and Fred's father. "He means business this time. If he wakes up before we get help, we're all dead." After I made the calls, she said, "Go get the other kids, put them in your room and shove the bed against your door."

That was the same bedroom door I had slammed on Donnie's fingers as he chased me through the house only a week before. I remember him yelling, "Ronnie, open the door. My fingers are caught in it." "You're crazy,

Donnie, you'll hurt me if I open that door," I yelled back. When I finally saw blood on the floor underneath the door, I realized he was serious. Our sibling rivalry was extreme at times, especially when we released all our pent up anger on each other. Kenny and Debbie were stuck in the middle of our rivalry and many times they caught the brunt of our anger.

Fred's dad was a retired Methodist minister, and he knew that Fred's drinking was getting out of hand. In spite of Fred's behavior, he and his family were highly respected in their upper-middle-class world. We always had the feeling that Fred felt we were misfits in his perfect family.

Fred's dad responded to my call and arrived quickly, even though it seemed like hours before he got there. Fred was still passed out on the bedroom floor. As Fred's dad went in to talk to him, the police surrounded the house. It was torture for all of us, huddling together in my room. I don't remember exactly what happened next and neither do the others. For me, it remains a blur of fear. Whatever happened that night was a taboo subject between us for many years, and we each were left alone with our nightmares.

We moved out of Fred's home that night and never returned. Although Fred never lived with us again, thoughts of him still lingered in our painful memories. For months after that awful night, Fred would call on the phone and threaten to come and kidnap Debbie. Many nights Donnie and I sat behind locked doors with baseball bats, waiting for him to fulfill his threats. Not long after that time, Fred was killed in a lone car accident. He was drunk. The memories of Fred's drunkenness haunted our lives for years.

My life turned towards total rebellion after Fred died. I remember as a young child vehemently proclaiming my disgust for alcohol and drugs. But by age thirteen, I was consistently violating my own rules. During the next four years, I had frequent episodes of heavy alcohol and drug use. I also created a "freak" or "hippie" image through my clothes, music, language and behavior.

When I was fifteen, my mother married John. His was a world where intelligence, higher education and cultural pursuits were valued. John was a successful and socially prominent person in our community, and he saw my life-style as a threat to his social standing. John and I represented two different worlds which were often in conflict. I was living in obvious rebellion to him and all he represented. His opera music and my rock music didn't mix. John's conformity and my divergent behavior were like oil and water. His martinis and my marijuana represented the two different approaches that we took to escape our reality and to medicate the pain of our lives.

The years from 1967 to 1970 were tough for both of us. Mother and "Mr. John" (as he had asked us to address him) did everything they could to try to bring me under their control. The more they tried, the more I rebelled. Our family struggle was a microcosm of the general societal unrest in the late sixties. The emerging hippie culture, anti-war demonstrations and the Civil Rights riots were all a part of that era. Obviously, ours was not the only family engaged in a conflict.

I ran away countless times before I finally managed to leave home for good at the age of 16. During those years I raised "hell," running the streets all night, stealing to survive, using people and drugs at will. I was expelled from school and sat for hours sniffing glue or gasoline fumes or taking trips of frightful fantasies on the acid wings of LSD. I slept in the woods or in old cars. I panhandled for quarters in malls and on street corners. I even went to jail—all in a desperate effort to fill the void in my life.

When I left North Carolina at 16, I headed for the party life in Florida. I was still searching for something but didn't know what. I had no contact with anyone in my family, and for months they didn't know where I was. I also didn't have any friends. Gradually, I began to realize I was not going to survive very long the way I was behaving. Living in Florida didn't change anything. Running and making geographical changes no longer helped me escape reality. I was empty, and I knew it. I hated the painful memories of my past, the emptiness of my present and the frightening thoughts of the future. I was headed nowhere.

It was then that I met Bill, a black heroin addict from Harlem, New York. Neither of us had any idea where we were going. His life appeared to be as empty as mine. We decided to flip the only remaining quarter we had to determine where to go next. We agreed that if the quarter came up heads, we would go west to Los Angeles. If it came up tails, we would go north to Toronto, Canada. The quarter landed on tails and off we went, hitchhiking our way toward Canada in October.

It took us two days to get through South Georgia. The people of Georgia didn't particularly like hippies or druggies at that time, and it was difficult to hitch a ride. Our first night out, a sheriff from Marshall County picked us up. He threatened to put us in his jail and never let us out if we ever stepped foot in his territory again. He then literally dropped us at the county line, swearing explicitly about worthless hippies, draft dodgers and blacks.

That night we slept in an abandoned house just over the county line. The next day we got a ride from a black man who was headed for Macon, Georgia. It wasn't where we wanted to go, but we hoped it was a ride in the right direction.

When we arrived in Macon, the man let us off on the main street in the heart of the black neighborhood. Here we were, two long-haired hippies, stuck in the middle of the black section of Macon, Georgia, in 1970. Bill was a mixture of Puerto Rican and Black American. He sported an afro and had light skin. His "fro" must have stuck out eighteen inches from his scalp and I could have sworn it was full of roaches. We had no money and no clothes except for the poncho and jeans we were wearing. My pants were tied together down the sides with pieces of leather and shoestrings. We were barefoot and had not bathed in weeks.

Several months before, Bill had stopped at a rock festival outside of Macon on his way south to Jacksonville. While he was there, he had met an unusual man whose name he happened to remember. We bummed a dime, found the man's number and called his house. He agreed to come pick us up and let us stay in his home for the night.

Bob was different from anyone I had ever met. I expected a hippie van to pull up with the sounds of blaring rock music coming out of the windows. Bill hadn't told me that this man was "straight" and even "preppie." Bob drove a conservative Chevrolet. He sported a short, neat haircut and wore slacks, a shirt with a button-down collar and penny loafers. I thought I left that world behind me in North Carolina and wondered why Bill called this nerd.

Bob introduced himself with a warmth I hadn't detected in a voice for years. We soon arrived at his two-story home in the inner city of Macon. I later learned the house was in the process of being restored to the glory it had known almost a century before. As I entered the house, I was met with the mouth-watering aroma of home-fried chicken. Sarah, Bob's wife, was in the kitchen preparing biscuits, mashed potatoes and gravy, green beans and fried chicken—my favorite meal. My mouth almost hit the floor when I realized she was preparing this for us. I had not eaten a real meal in months. The closest I had come to home-fried chicken was retrieving throw-aways from dumpsters after closing time at Kentucky Fried Chicken restaurants.

After dinner Bob offered Bill and me the opportunity to take baths. I didn't have to wonder why. After months, I was ready for one. My bath that night felt how I thought heaven must feel. Bill and I even had our own bedrooms with double beds and fresh sheets.

I fell asleep while trying to figure out Bob and Sarah's angle. What were they after? Where would Bill and I go tomorrow? In spite of their hospitality, I was still suspicious. At dinner, I had learned that Bob recently graduated from Duke Divinity School in Durham, North Carolina, with a Master's Degree in Theology. "Mr. John," my stepfather, had also graduated from Duke University, and his father now taught there.

The breakfast Sarah served was as good and as plentiful as supper the night before. Afterwards, Bob and Sarah invited us to stay with them for awhile. They told us they felt we needed to get on our feet before we continued our trip. I could not believe what I was hearing—much less what I was experiencing. I thought maybe I was dreaming, and I wondered how something so good could happen to me.

None of us could have imagined what was to transpire in the years ahead. That sincere offer of hospitality turned my life around. Bob and Sarah did not appear to be intimidated by my life-style, and they didn't try to intimidate me by theirs. Their ground rules were simple and fair—mutual respect and no violations of their drug-free environment. Although I didn't know it at the time, Bob and Sarah were my first encounter with people in a Christ-centered recovery community.

The second night there, Bill and I went over to the campus of Mercer University, a Baptist college, and obtained some dynamite LSD. Without giving it a further thought, we did what any good drug addicts would do;

we took it. But the moment I swallowed that acid, something happened to me that had never happened before. I freaked out.

For the first time in my life, I felt guilt and sorrow for letting someone down. Bob and Sarah were being good to us, and I was doing this behind their backs. I went straight back to their house and told Bob what I had done. Bill got as hot as a firecracker at me. Bob's response was consistent with everything else I had seen him do in the two days I had known him. He was the first person to ever tell me that he understood and that he would forgive me. "We'll talk further in the morning," he said as he left the room and went to bed.

Bill was so mad at me that he did everything he could to cause me to have a "bad trip." For reasons I will never understand, it did not work the way he hoped. Instead, my "bad trip" was the first encounter I had with God. In my fear of losing my mind, I asked God for help. I didn't bargain, just asked for his help in my life. What I didn't realize was that God had been reaching out to me ever since the sheriff in South Georgia had kicked us out of his county and headed us away from Toronto and toward Macon.

Bill really thought I had flipped out when he heard me praying, and it wasn't long before he left us. I saw him once much later in Jackson Square Park in the French Quarter of New Orleans, Louisiana. He looked the same—maybe even a little harder than he had before. I witnessed to Bill that day about the God I had met the morning after my last acid trip.

That day was indeed the beginning of a new life for me. Bob came to me first thing in the morning and told me I could stay with him and Sarah only if I was willing to follow their ground rules. I looked him straight in the eyes (which was also a first) and asked, "What makes you tick? Something is really different about you, Bob. You really do seem to care. You seem to have purpose and meaning in your life. If I didn't know better, I'd think you really knew where you were headed. You and Sarah have something I want."

Bob's answer was simple and straightforward: "Jesus Christ is our Lord and Savior. We love him and we follow him. He fills the empty places and gives our lives direction, purpose and meaning." He told me I needed to ask Christ to come into my life, to cleanse me and to become my Lord and Savior. That's exactly what I did and, true to his promise, Christ has worked in my life in the same way he works in the lives of Bob and Sarah. That day I entered the first stage of my Christ-centered recovery.

Bob and Sarah did not preach to me, but simply lived their faith. Their example filled me with my own desire for a better life. Never again did I use drugs or think about suicide. I lived with Bob and Sarah for nearly two years, during which time they nurtured my new life in Christ. When I first met Bob, I didn't know he was a Methodist pastor creating a parish from the inner city streets of Macon. Nor did I know I was their first project.

During my stay with them, Bob, Sarah and I moved into a 33 room antebellum mansion where we developed what was later called "His House." In the 1970s, His House became a street outreach, halfway house, crisis intervention center and worshiping community composed of street people.

During those early years in Macon, Georgia, God used many people to help me establish my new life in Christ. They became my first Christ-centered recovery community. Today, 19 years later, many of these same people still worship God together and reach out to nurture people just like me.

After two years with Bob and Sarah, some of my old thoughts, feelings and behaviors returned. I began to tantalize myself with the notion that I could do my own thing and still follow Christ. I could not have been more wrong. It was during this time that I met the woman who would become my first wife. She was a senior at Wesleyan who came to His House to write a sociology term paper about the "hippies" who were being transformed there. I became the principal focus of her research. I must have intrigued her, perhaps because my life was so different from hers. She was from an aristocratic military family in Augusta, Georgia.

Within days of our meeting, I announced to my friends at His House that we were to be married. They promptly told me that our relationship was too new to be anything more than lustful and that possibly it was not God's best plan for us. I wondered how they could know this and questioned their right to tell me what to do. I left His House, determined to be my own person and do my own thing. After all, I was 19, and I knew what was best for me. How I deceived myself! Not only did I not know what was best for me, I didn't consider what was best for my future wife.

In June, she moved back to Augusta to be with her dying mother. I spent the summer with my family before entering college in the fall. This was the first time I had been with them in over three years. When I left home I was a drug addict and a high school dropout. When I returned, I was sober and had a high school diploma along with a new faith in Christ.

Both of my fiancee's parents died of cancer within the next year. I transferred to Augusta College after my first quarter at Young Harris College. I was almost 20 years old, and I had received my first call to pastor three small churches about 20 miles outside of Augusta. We were married the next spring and moved into the church parsonage.

Things were looking up. I thought I was living proof that I knew what was best for me. During this period, I believed I could live partly in Christ-centered recovery and partly in self-help recovery. That precipitated a whole new set of problems for me. I became a double-minded person and ended up unstable in all ways, seriously compromising my recovery.

My relationship with my wife began to deteriorate as I became more and more self-centered. Both of us professed to believe in Christ and attended church together, but we lived according to our own youthful lusts. My old resentments, fears, insecurities and difficulties with intimacy began to cause problems in our relationship.

I began to relate to my wife in the same way I had with my family of origin. We never communicated; I manipulated her by using all of the sick patterns I had learned from my childhood role models. The only difference was that I was self-righteous and in deep denial about the dysfunctional behaviors that developed in our relationship.

For the next five years I lived the life of a hypocrite. As a young pastor, many people thought of me as a rising star in the Methodist ministry. I pictured myself as their token hippie convert. The truth was, I was actually playacting even more during those years than I had been before I accepted Christ. I said one thing, but did another. My marriage was miserable, and I immersed myself in pornography. I used, conned, manipulated and emotionally abused my wife. I cheated my way through school because I was too undisciplined to study. For me, school was a necessary evil and a prerequisite for achieving my goal of being ordained as a Methodist minister.

I stopped asking Jesus for his opinion. Instead, I preached my own interpretation of his opinions. I quenched the Holy Spirit within me by my sinful and hypocritical life. I used tales of "spiritual" experiences to gain more attention. I was driven to prove myself to the father I never had, to my mother and "Mr. John," to Bob and Sarah and to all the other people in Macon.

Most of all, I needed to prove to myself that I was somebody. I was totally wrapped up in this deception. I carefully shut everyone else out of my life, especially Jesus. I know now that in spite of the way I treated him, Jesus never abandoned me.

Finally, my wife had taken all she could. Her incessant tears, confrontations and pleading with me to face my problems and get help fell on deaf ears. As far as I was concerned, she was the one with the problems. In my opinion, all she needed to do was submit to me and accept me as I was. As a matter of fact, I thought she was darn lucky to be married to me. In reality, she was married to someone in serious trouble, but I couldn't see the reality of any of my pain until she finally decided to divorce me and get me out of her life.

The hurt and rejection I felt over the divorce were severe. I went into a grieving depression that lasted for months. At first, I tried to change her mind by pestering, threatening and begging her to reconcile with me. When that didn't work, I reacted with anger and cockiness. "I don't need her anyway," I thought. "I don't need anyone." Of course, I was too "religious" to admit my confusion and anger toward God. Somehow I convinced myself that living with her was limiting my ambitions anyway. I concluded that I was much better off without her.

It was then that I began to behave in much the same way as I had in my teenage years. The difference was that I hid it better this time. I was a pastor and a pillar in the United Methodist Church. I had my "religion" and my career to protect. Bars, strip joints, porno flicks and one night stands became a part of my double life. I was a repulsive character, especially to myself.

Finally, I began to see my depraved, sick state of being. I hit bottom for the first time since my conversion experience seven years prior. At this point I realized that I had been subverting the Holy Spirit within me by trying to manage my own life. Jesus was no longer my Lord and Savior; I was. Unfortunately, it took a failed marriage and hitting bottom to convince me that my only hope was through an honest self-examination, repentance and total submission to Christ as Lord.

I spent hours weeping with sorrow over the condition of my life. I truly wanted to be clear, clean, whole and functional. But there was a definite price tag. God required that I be honest with him, myself and others and that I return to Christ-centered recovery. Gradually, I began to see that I could only be healed if I made some major changes in my life. I had to face up to the wrongs I had committed, accept my responsibility and make restitution. I was guided by God to:

— Ask my ex-wife to forgive me.

— Resign from my pastorate and make amends to my church.

— Resign from graduate school and return my college degree with an admission to the president of all my years of cheating. (The president returned my diploma with a stern admonition and a word of encouragement about the new-found wisdom he saw in my confession.)

— Contact all those persons I had ever hurt, stolen from, or abused. Make restitution to them by asking for their forgiveness and offering to pay back, with interest, any money involved.

— Become a functioning part of a Christ-centered recovery community and return to ministry only when I had made considerable progress in recovery.

— Spend large blocks of time in structured meditation and Bible study.

— Seek out a willing pastor or other person who would be a disciple and counselor for me and who would support my recovery.

During my time of repentance, I committed to my Lord Jesus that I would give my life over to righteousness; no longer would I allow sin to be my master and me its slave. Through prayer, I came to believe that my future could be better than my past. I knew that if I did exactly what the Lord required of me, I would have another chance.

It was at this point that God called me to move to Titusville, Florida, and to serve in Pastor Peter Lord's ministry. One of the associate pastors there, Pastor Robbie Goss, agreed to take me under his wing and help me work through the instructions God had given me for repentance. At the same time, I was involved in a ministry training program under Pastor Lord and the staff of Park Avenue Baptist Church. This opportunity proved to be an extremely important step in my recovery in Christ.

While in Titusville, I met Janis, the woman who was to become my wife. We submitted our relationship to God and to our pastors. This was my first honest relationship with a woman. During our engagement, our pastors helped us prepare for our life together. This period was also crucial to my restoration in Christ. Janis and I were married in June of 1980. She has since become the Lord's agent for change in my life. Janis supports me and speaks honestly with me in a loving and caring way. She walks beside me in Christ-centered recovery as we both seek his will for our lives.

Although we had been told it was unlikely that Janis could carry a pregnancy to full term, the Lord miraculously blessed us with our first daughter, Erin Joy, in December, 1981. In May, 1989, God generously gave us another daughter, Amy Elizabeth.

Being a father and husband, with Christ as head of our home, has been an indescribable joy for me. Becoming a cooperative, energetic participant in his community of recovery has become the single greatest factor in my personal faith pilgrimage.

Pastors Lord and Goss encouraged me, after working through the process of repentance and training, to pursue the ministry to which God had called me. They introduced me to Mickey Evans, founder and director of Dunklin Memorial Camp, a Christian alcohol and drug rehabilitation center, church, retreat center and city of refuge in Okeechobee, Florida. In his infinite grace, Christ called me to serve as pastor in this special recovery community. How my family and I grew with our brothers and sisters in this loving group! They spoke the truth in love when we needed it, prayed for us continually, laughed and cried with us, helped us and held us accountable for doing God's will.

The call to pastor at Dunklin was a unique opportunity to see God's grace at work in my life. He helped me minister to others in the very areas where I had been most comforted by him. Only through my time of breaking, repentance and restoration could the door to servanthood be opened for me. This opportunity to serve the body of Christ fulfilled a deep need in my heart and gave me a chance to become an ambassador of Christ again—this time with integrity.

The most important steps in my recovery where I clearly experienced the Holy Spirit's healing presence were through:

— Reconciliation of my relationship with God.

— Reconciliation of my relationships with my father, mother and stepfather.

— Reconciliation of my relationships with my brothers and sister.

— Restoration of my vocation and calling in Christ.

— Healing from chemical addiction, unhealthy relationships and other self-destructive behaviors.

This is how I grew up and became an adult. It is the story of my recovery from a painful childhood to a healthy adult life in Christ-centered recovery. I no longer blame the people around me for my problems. Some of them are aware of my struggles and are encouraging my recovery. I am now able to realize that all who have been a part of my life are significant to me. All but one person graciously granted me permission to share my story of recovery in this book. My first wife was not consulted, and therefore is not referred to by name.

I have recently become aware that during my troubled years, my grandmother prayed daily for my recovery. This awareness has helped me to understand the many spiritual interventions that protected me and guided me into Christ-centered recovery. My grandmother spent the last years of her life suffering with Alzheimer's disease, but even in that debilitating condition she focused her life unselfishly on praying for those she loved and to whom she could no longer relate.

Christ has taken my life from childishness to childlikeness, dysfunction to function and woundedness to wholeness. In Christ, I now have a purpose in life and hope for the future. The good news is that through Christ, we can all be healed. May your journey be blessed, and may you enjoy the fruits of the Holy Spirit in your life.

Individual Exercise

- Identify the major traumas in your life during childhood. _____

  _____
  _____
  _____
  _____
  _____
  _____

- Describe the major traumas in your life during adolescence. _____

  _____
  _____
  _____
  _____
  _____
  _____

- Describe the major traumas in your life during adulthood. _____

  _____
  _____
  _____
  _____
  _____
  _____

- What destructive behavior patterns did you adopt to cope with the dysfunction in your home? _____

_____

_____

_____

_____

_____

_____

- What motivated you to seek recovery? _____

_____

_____

_____

_____

_____

_____

- Pray for guidance from Jesus to help you in your recovery journey and write your reflections. _____

_____

_____

_____

_____

_____

_____

Recovery Tool: Journal Writing

A journal is a notebook reserved for recording our experiences, ideas and reflections. As such, it can become a valuable recovery tool when used to write down insights about our recovery. A journal is not meant to be shared with anyone; it is a personal means to record our spiritual pilgrimage. It can become one of our most treasured possessions. Taking the time to write every day can provide us with a vital documentation of Christ's work in our lives.

The Holy Spirit is working in us and through us daily and, as we write in our journal, we learn to pay attention to our thoughts, feelings and behaviors. Our transformation comes from within, and as we experience and record the pain and joy of our recovery, God reveals even greater insights to us.

Journal writing is potentially the cornerstone of our individual program of personal growth. It enables us to open and expand our thinking in many directions. Keeping journals has been a time-honored practice from the confessions of St. Augustine to the spiritual diaries of the Quakers, or Society of Friends. These journals were the precursors of modern psychological and spiritual workbooks. The goal of a recovery journal is neither literary creation nor religious soul-searching, but a dynamic and self-transforming observance of our walk with the Lord.

Following are some important points to remember while journaling:

— Develop a routine of recording in your journal on a regular basis.

— Date each entry.

— Describe the main impressions that come to mind when reflecting on an experience.

— Make entries as succinct and objective as possible. Avoid analyzing an experience in great detail or wallowing in self-pity.

— Relax and pay attention to feelings about the experience, not just thoughts or descriptions.

— Recognize a feeling or an insight, write it down and move on to the next activity without dwelling on it.

- Make note of images that surface during writing, as they can provide material for future journaling.
- Read previous journal entries periodically. Add new feelings and insights as supplemental notes to the original entry.

Group Exercise

Refer to page 177 for the *Week One* meeting format.

● In what ways have you tried to help yourself recover that have not worried? _____

_____

_____

_____

_____

_____

_____

● What motivated you to join a Christ-centered recovery group? _____

_____

_____

_____

_____

_____

_____

● What areas of your life are causing you the most difficulty today? Explain. _____

_____

_____

_____

_____

_____

_____

- Share a meaningful experience in using the journal as part of your recovery process. _____

  _____

  _____

  _____

  _____

  _____

  _____

  _____

- Respond briefly to the question **"Who Am I?"** _____

  _____

  _____

  _____

  _____

  _____

  _____

  _____

- What is your prayer request for yourself or others? _____

  _____

  _____

  _____

  Complete the following *Family Group Prayer Requests*.

  _____ is praying for me.

  I am praying for _____ and his/her prayer request is

  _____

  _____

  _____

Chapter Two

Pain Insulators

. . . .

Many of us try in vain to insulate ourselves from the suffering that surrounds us. We tend to live in a fantasy world presenting ourselves as happy, well-adjusted individuals. In so doing, we set ourselves outside of our own reality and defeat the purpose of pain in our lives. Pain is a symptom of "dis-ease", a sign that something is wrong. One of its purposes is to help us see our lives as they really are and accept the need for recovery.

Billions of dollars are spent annually to assist this cover-up, as we legally and illegally medicate our pain with mood-altering substances and addictive behaviors. We pursue creature comforts, toys and all kinds of buffers to further insulate us from reality. We often define success by the number of "things" we possess.

To perpetuate the influence of these pain insulators, we may extend our belief in their "magic" and relax our standards of behavior. We indulge in the fantasy that these insulators make our world a better and less painful place in which to live. The truth is, it only works for a short while—in our individual lives and in our society.

As a people, we have allowed ourselves to be part of the great "American dream," which passes on the pain insulators from one generation to the next. However, the American dream has turned into a nightmare for many families. This nightmare leads us, through our denial, to place false value on money, power and other things of this world. Success is defined in these terms instead of in terms of wholeness and health. Further, the American dream supports the fantasy that the truly successful are not in pain.

We've all watched the great American dream, with its negative influences, affect the lives of many people. The model of a healthy, Christ-centered family is in danger of being totally consumed by the lustful, ravenous appetites that are part of our society. As we pass this condition to each successive generation, we move further out of touch with reality.

An essential step in breaking through this destructive illusion is to redefine success. We look to the Bible to reveal Jesus' ideas about success and see that his definition of it is very different from ours. For example, when asked what was the greatest commandment in the law, "*Jesus replied: 'Love the Lord your God with all your heart and with all your soul and with all your mind. This is the first and greatest commandment. And the second is like it: Love your neighbor as yourself.'*" MATTHEW 22:37-39 (NIV).

Jesus places the highest priority on loving God, ourselves and other people instead of loving things and using people, as we often do in our society. As we live out his message and reflect God's love in our own lives we achieve a different kind of success—the success of being loving, functioning individuals who face our pain and work through it. Only by our strong example, not by our talk, can we expose the dangers of the American dream.

Too often, lack of proper preparation for adulthood is a direct result of our fathers and mothers believing this myth. Parents who are at home infrequently have little time for training their children for adult life. Many parents are turning more of that responsibility over to day care centers, schools, the media and their children's peers.

These parents are out in the marketplace, bringing home money and material things. This material "bacon" is not necessarily what we need or want; it can clog the veins of our heart which depletes our family's vitality. It can weigh us down with the fat of things, leaving us lethargic and unresponsive to one another.

This desire for material success can give rise to the insideous diseases and behaviors attacking American family life and perpetuating generations of pain and dysfunction. Among these diseases and behaviors are addiction to drugs or alcohol, sexual abuse, violence, eating disorders and unhealthy relationships. The list keeps growing.

Most children do not need more bacon. They need parents who reflect Christ's priorities of loving God and extending that love to themselves and others. Recovery doesn't mean knowing how to bring home bigger and better bacon; it means being prepared and mature enough to reflect God's love in a healthy way and to relate to others who are also motivated by that love. When we are able to do this, we can interact with others without needing to control or manipulate them. We learn to love people and use things as Jesus taught us.

In our efforts to insulate ourselves from pain, many of us lose our true or private selves. Therapists often say that our true identities have become swallowed up by our public selves. It is not hard to imagine how a public image, created in an effort to fulfill the American dream, emerges as a facade. Many of us believe wearing this mask is essential for our acceptance and approval.

Frequently, we present ourselves to others in the image of models in advertisements rather than in the image of God. The demand for these public persona can lead to the devaluation of our true selves. We may end up not knowing, loving, or even liking who we truly are. The creation of these divergent selves is tragic. We have fabricated a warped likeness of ourselves, and we model that behavior to our youth. Through it all, we lose sight of Jesus, whose image we were created to reflect.

Jesus is the representation in human form of God's loving nature. During his life on earth, he gave us messages that provide a model of what our true character can be. Christ shows us what God values and what we should value. His image represents the standard of morality that we are intended to reflect and the guide for relating to each other. Without that image, we could not know how to lovingly communicate or achieve maturity in recovery.

Many therapists tell us there are no absolutes or norms with which to compare ourselves in our pain-filled society. Christ can fill this gap if we change our focus from the "things" of this world and begin to follow his example of healthy, loving behavior. He knew that our greatest rewards would come from our relationship with God, ourselves and others.

Our pain-filled society also suffers because many Christians misrepresent God and hide his image. Sometimes the church focuses on the judgment and wrath of God and forgets about the love and forgiveness given by him through Christ. Another misrepresentation of God is a lack of distinction between woundedness and sin. The wounds we sustained while growing up in a dysfunctional home were beyond our control and not a direct result of our own actions, but we often felt guilty anyway. On the other hand, sin is a willful act for which one is accountable and for which it is appropriate to feel guilty. Understanding the difference between woundedness and sin is extremely important for adult children because of the severe wounds inflicted upon us.

The church has often mistakenly presented all problems as sin and been self-righteous and judgmental about sinners. Consideration is not always given to woundedness as a reason for our problems. The church has often portrayed God as vengeful and angry, wanting to punish us rather than show us the love and forgiveness that are ours because Christ died on the cross for our sins.

It is important to understand that our behavior is not the only basis for our pain. The wounds we have suffered also cause pain and they must be healed in order for us to achieve wholeness. The lack of distinction between woundedness and sin has led many Christians to believe that "turning from sin" is the solution to recovery. This is simply not true, either from a therapeutic or from a biblical standpoint. We also need to heal our wounds and change our thinking about how to react to people and events.

Many of the injuries we suffered in dysfunctional childhood homes were caused by the actions of the adults in our lives. It is often in reaction to our wounds that we sin by drinking excessively or behaving violently. In turn, we pass on to our children the injuries inflicted upon us.

Our society is in need of loving, forgiving, fully present and responsible parents or caregivers who provide models for functional family life. The self-righteous, superficial, rigid and legalistic attitudes in our institutionalized religions often serve only to drive a deeper wedge between the painful world and Christ, who died for our salvation. There surely are as many painful homes inside of the institutional religious structure as there are outside of it.

Prior to the industrial revolution, the family had priority in every culture. The family worked together as a unit and played a major role in shaping society's values. It was the place where skills for adult life were modeled and learned. It was where we developed God-given belief and value systems, moral standards, work ethics and relational skills. The healthy family system represented discipline and character development which enabled children to mature into healthy, functional adults.

The family unit seems to have lost its influence over the crucial issues in our society. It appears that each generation is degenerating to some degree. In many families, the home is no longer the place where skills for successful adult life are modeled and taught.

Along with the demise of the traditional family unit has come the decreasing influence of the church. It is very difficult for the church to have more impact on shaping lives than individuals and their families do. The local church is only as weak or as strong as her individual family units. In our contemporary society, both the family and the church have a greatly reduced influence in shaping each generation.

In my own observation of working with wounded people, the examples of family and church are being greatly overshadowed by outside distractions that are essentially destructive. Some of the predominant distractions that have a negative influence are: television, movies, newspapers, magazines and other media, drugs, alcohol, pornography, rock music and peer groups.

The list of negative influences in our society seems to be growing with the passing of time. If the grief we see is any evidence, ours is certainly a generation in pain. We seem to be hurting with more intensity as each generation passes the damage on to the next. Many of us thought that the decade of the sixties would be unparalleled in its pain. The difficulties over civil rights, Vietnam, hippies and drugs were intense.

However, it seems the struggles of the seventies and eighties are similar if not greater than the strife in the sixties. Life in the nineties is difficult to contemplate. The future of the human family may even depend on our taking a closer look at the pain in our own lives and the ways in which we can be models of recovery.

Substance abuse and compulsive behavior are prevalent in our society. Alcoholism has contributed to untold loss of life and increased the pain and suffering of those involved in and affected by it. The birth of drug-addicted children is alarming and can negatively affect their families and society as a whole. Crime, divorce, desertion, eating disorders, sexual molestation of children and physical abuse of women and children are all grave concerns. The effects of neglect, denial of feelings, workaholism, rejection, fear of failure and living in a performance-oriented rather than people-oriented society are likewise damaging.

Our hope lies in recognizing that God, reflected in Christ, is the true model for how we are to behave as individuals and interact within our communities. When our priority is one of reflecting a loving, protecting and nurturing God in our lives, we have a chance to make a difference in succeeding generations.

Parents who are emotionally available to their children and can provide tangible, visible images of the character and ways of Christ are critically needed in our society. Otherwise, each generation is faced with having an increasingly difficult time learning how to live in love and, thus, in community. Our only hope is to restore the loving, compassionate and responsible model of parenthood that is revealed through Christ to the family, church and society.

All of these conditions contribute to the increasing numbers of adult children in our society today. It is through recognition of this condition, and a willingness to effect change, that we can provide hope for those who are suffering.

Individual Exercise

- List the ways in which you insulate yourself from pain. _____

  _____

  _____

  _____

  _____

  _____

  _____

  _____

- What factors do you think contribute to your success as a person? __

  _____

  _____

  _____

  _____

  _____

  _____

  _____

- What is the difference between your public self and your true self?
  Explain. _____

  _____

  _____

  _____

  _____

  _____

  _____

  _____

- How has the American dream affected your life? _____

  _____

  _____

  _____

  _____

  _____

  _____

  _____

- Describe your childhood relationship with your mother. _____

  _____

  _____

  _____

  _____

  _____

  _____

  _____

- Describe your childhood relationship with your father. _____

  _____

  _____

  _____

  _____

  _____

  _____

  _____

Recovery Tool: Humility

Humility is an important element in our recovery process. It keeps the door open to the grace of God, which gives us the power to achieve permanent change. "....*clothe yourselves with humility toward one another, because, 'God opposes the proud but gives grace to the humble.' Humble yourselves, therefore, under God's mighty hand, that he may lift you up in due time. Cast all your anxiety on him because he cares for you.*" 1 PETER 5:4-7 (NIV).

Three basic elements of humility that can aid us in recovery are:

Being willing to ask for and accept help.

It is important to seek help from God and from other people and not rely only on our own strengths and resources. When we turn over all our cares to God, he manages our burdens far beyond our own capacity to do so.

Being willing to learn.

We need to be willing to examine ourselves and gain the self-understanding that is crucial to our being truthful with God, ourselves and others throughout our journey to recovery.

Being willing to see ourselves from God's perspective.

It is important to recognize our significance to God and our unique place in creation, as well as our insignificance in the affairs of the world and our powerlessness to change by ourselves. When we keep our pride or our low self-esteem from interfering, we can see ourselves as God sees us.

Group Exercise

Refer to page 181 for the *Week Two* meeting format.

- Why is humility necessary as part of your recovery? _____

_____

_____

_____

_____

_____

_____

- How do the wounds of your past affect your life today? What are you willing to do to heal these wounds? _____

_____

_____

_____

_____

_____

- What pain insulators do you use as a way to protect yourself from situations that are troublesome to you? _____

_____

_____

_____

_____

_____

● What standards of behavior do you believe Jesus modeled for us? __

_____

_____

_____

_____

_____

_____

_____

● Share a meaningful experience in using the journal as part of your recovery process. _____

_____

_____

_____

_____

_____

_____

_____

● What is your prayer request for yourself or others? _____

_____

_____

_____

_____

Complete the following *Family Group Prayer Requests*.

_____ is praying for me.

I am praying for _____ and his/her prayer request is

_____

_____

_____

_____

Chapter Three

Stunted Growth

. . . .

*W*hen we are no longer able to endure our pain, it is time to look at our symptoms, which are usually consistent and definable in adults who were raised in dysfunctional homes. This is because our growth was stunted, impaired or interrupted in some way. Stunted growth occurs either when we are deprived of something that is vital to our growth or when we experience abuse during development. Each stage of development in our lives is an important transition in the maturing process.

At all stages, children must be loved, cared for, affirmed and guided in order to develop into mature adults. If we are abused or deprived of what we need as children, we age chronologically but do not mature emotionally. When we reach adulthood, we are actually children trapped in adult bodies. We are often referred to as adult children. This book is intended to help us as adult children to recover from the traumas of our past. It is designed to teach us how to "grow up and become an adult."

Looking back on our past, many of us might say, "If only I could be a child again." Wouldn't it be great to have a second chance at being a child living in a happy and functional home? Who wouldn't love the opportunity of not paying bills or not having to work 40 to 60 hours a week. Imagine spending many weeks playing or on vacation!

For too many of us, childhood was not happy, and childhood memories may not always bring images of carefree and joyful times. Instead, we may have painful memories, fears and a general feeling of sadness that surface when we reflect on our childhood. For some of us, it may be a blur, marked by severe memory loss. For others, a wealth of negative emotions may overshadow any pleasant memories we might have.

In 1 Corinthians 13:11 (NIV), we read, "*When I was a child, I talked like a child, I thought like a child, I reasoned like a child...*" A symptom of our present painful condition is that many of us cannot understand this biblical description. As children, we didn't have the opportunity to talk, think, or reason as a child. So we did not experience the maturing process necessary for becoming an adult and putting childish ways behind us.

When our growth is stunted, we may be unable to function in critical areas of our lives. For example, we may be mentally and emotionally unstable. Some of us may not be able to achieve and maintain healthy relationships or sustain physical and spiritual health. We may be chronologically and biologically adult, but still children emotionally. We may have physically mature bodies but lack many of the skills necessary for functional adult living. As adult children, our development may have been impaired by growing up in a home where appropriate communication and nurture were absent.

Those of us who have not experienced childhood properly may not be able to put childish behavior behind us. We may feel frustration at not being able to handle adult responsibilities and relationships. We may wear ourselves out trying to encourage growth or wholeness in ourselves or others. Some of us may feel stuck in the same problems year after year, always hoping and believing "things will get better."

The pain of a negative childhood lingers with us long into adulthood. It doesn't just go away with the passing of time. The inability to function in adult life doesn't automatically correct itself. To become whole, we need to define and deal with the issues of our past that have inhibited our growth and kept us stuck in the trauma of a painful childhood.

If our parents suffered from some sort of dysfunction, whether it was alcoholism or some other condition, their ability to be healthy role models was impaired. Many of our parents were wounded because they were raised in painful homes. Whatever the circumstances, we were not able to develop in a normal, God-intended fashion. Instead, we began to live in reaction to the behavior of those around us.

Most of us were not even aware that we were not maturing properly. We probably assumed we were as normal as everyone else, but we were usually left wondering what "normal" might be. If there were no healthy adults around to aid us in discerning what was appropriate and what was inappropriate, we had no measure by which to assess our own experiences. Yes, some pain is normal—some conflicts in families are normal—some childhood responsibility is normal—some negative thoughts and feelings are normal—some fears and concerns are normal. In our vain attempts to figure out what was acceptable, we might have asked ourselves some of the following questions:

— Is it normal to see my parents fighting all the time?

— Is it normal to have to scream to be heard?

— Is it normal to be left alone, taking care of my younger brothers and sisters, when I am only seven years old?

— Is it normal to do most of the cooking, laundry and cleaning when I am only nine years old?

— Is it normal to bleed after I have been punished?

— Is it normal to have to put mommy or daddy to bed?

— Is it normal to have to tell daddy's boss that he can't come to work again because he is sick?

— Is it normal to have different men in mommy's bedroom while daddy is gone?

— Is it normal to eat mostly junk food at mealtimes?

— Is it normal to have to call an ambulance for mommy after daddy came home and yelled at her for a while and then left again?

— Is it normal to seldom be allowed to play?

— Is it normal to have to sit up at night with a baseball bat waiting for my stepfather to return because he has threatened to kill the whole family?

— Is it normal at age eleven to have to attack my stepfather when he is drunk to keep him from hurting my mommy or my sister?

— Is it normal for daddy to leave home and never come back?

— Is it normal to feel ashamed of my family?

— Is it normal to want to leave home because no one will talk to me?

— Is it normal to feel numb, no matter what happens?

— Is it normal to think it's my fault when my sister dies?

— Is it normal to feel guilty when mom and dad break up?

— Is it normal to feel that I am a bad person because someone else treats me badly?

— Is it normal to wish I were somebody else's kid?

— Is it normal to wish I had not been born?

We may have been damaged by the crazy rules enforced in our parental homes, such as "don't talk," "don't trust," "don't feel." Negative behaviors like these hinder our growth rather than facilitate it. They can cause us to repress our emotions, which becomes devastating to us and to our relationships. Some of the crazy rules we might have learned are:

— Not to talk about our thoughts, preferences, desires, concerns, home life, or problems.

— To talk only about superficial or insignificant subjects.

— Not to trust anyone or anything. Sometimes we don't even trust ourselves.

— Not to trust that God is with us and truly loves us.

— To deny our feelings or become unaware of having them.

— To mask our feelings or call them by another name.

These rules may continue to govern our behavior as adults. They can help us to pretend that nothing unusual is happening and aid our relentless defense of past and present family systems. If we are going to recover, we need to replace the old crazy rules of our childhood with new life-affirming behaviors that enhance our growth.

While searching for wholeness through recovery, we can find clues in the Bible. MATTHEW 5:48 (NIV) refers to *"becoming perfect as our Heavenly Father is perfect,"* a sign of reaching toward maturity. ROMANS 8:29 (NIV) talks of *"being conformed to his likeness,"* a promise of growing into the fullness of Christ. And EPHESIANS 4:23 (NIV) stresses *"being made new in the attitude of our minds,"* a guideline for changing for the better. Using passages from Scripture in this way can help us see that turning to Christ in recovery as our support and guide enables us to grow and change.

Having been slowed down in our growth doesn't excuse us from the call to maturity and the realization of the wholeness we can find in Christ-centered recovery. In order to initiate our healing, it is important that we face our pain and understand our symptoms as adult children. Only then can we move on to functional adult living.

As an adult child, we may find ourselves struggling with many issues that are discomforting to us. The symptoms which are listed on the following page have been determined to be common among adult children.

Common Symptoms of Adult Children

— We are incapable of building and maintaining enduring, meaningful and intimate relationships with God, ourselves, or others.

— We find it difficult to trust ourselves or others in a deepening fashion; thus, it is hard for us to live by faith.

— We do not possess the skills or vocabulary necessary for the healthy communication of feelings, preferences, ideas, or needs.

— We do not know how to manage the inevitable stresses of life; we cannot easily play, relax, or rest.

— We do not possess all of the skills necessary to understand God's will in our lives.

— We are resistant to change.

— We are rigid and inflexible in our thoughts and actions.

— We lack the ability to grow spiritually and emotionally.

— We do not know how or where to seek help or to offer help to others.

— We do not know how to handle adult responsibilities and relationships.

— We often feel that we do not belong anywhere.

— We have difficulty developing healthy beliefs, morals and values.

— We have a strong need to be in control.

— We have difficulty following projects from beginning to end.

— We feel guilty when we stand up for ourselves.

— We give in to others instead of taking care of ourselves.

We may not necessarily exhibit all of the characteristics prevalent in adult children. However, any symptoms we do have must be identified and adequately addressed if we are to live as mature, healthy adults. These feelings and behaviors are the direct result of not having been given the foundation necessary for living as an adult. The realities of our childhood, however damaging they might have been, do not give us an excuse to reproduce the same symptoms in our own children.

Healing begins when we understand that God wants us to reach our full potential—to find fulfillment, maturity and wholeness. The Bible is filled with exhortations to grow, and when our God-ordained growth is stopped, we become a warped form of what God intended us to be. As we seek to become "adult" in every dimension of our lives, we begin to realize our potential for becoming whole spiritually, mentally, emotionally and physically. Christ-centered recovery enables us to discern God's will and to mature as quickly or as slowly as is right for each one of us.

While moving toward adulthood, toward being mature and whole in Christ, we become integrated and balanced, and our behavior begins to match our new belief system. Our personalities reflect our true selves, and we no longer pretend to be someone we are not. We stop imitating others and claim our own identity. Gradually we become secure enough to accept ourselves as we are and cease performing to please others.

The farther we progress in recovery, the more we recognize how much we can rely on the grace of God to empower us to meet the demands of our adult responsibilities and relationships. While making peace with our past and learning from it, we stop repeating our negative behaviors and try new, healthier ways of living.

As we begin to grow, we find ourselves "practicing what we preach." Our attitudes, thoughts, morals and values become the basis of our actions, and our behavior becomes more and more reflective of Christ. As adults in Christ we learn to give generously and receive graciously; we become blessings wherever we are instead of a drain on those around us. Being an adult in Christ calls us to reflect our deepening trust in God and his unconditional love.

Individual Exercise

- What questions about a normal childhood occurred to you as you read the list of questions in the chapter? _____

  _____

  _____

  _____

  _____

  _____

  _____

- Write down the major "crazy" rules that operated in your home of origin. _____

  _____

  _____

  _____

  _____

  _____

  _____

- How are these crazy rules operating in your life today? _____

  _____

  _____

  _____

  _____

  _____

- What are the major symptoms of stunted growth that you feel you display in your life now? _____

  _____

  _____

  _____

  _____

  _____

  _____

- List the two adult child symptoms that cause you the most amount of difficulty. Explain. _____

  _____

  _____

  _____

  _____

  _____

- List the two adult child symptoms that cause you the least amount of difficulty. Explain. _____

  _____

  _____

  _____

  _____

  _____

Recovery Tool: Prayer and Meditation

The following material, adapted from *The Twelve Steps—A Spiritual Journey*, can help us more effectively use prayer and meditation as a tool for recovery.

A daily regimen of prayer and meditation makes it clear that relief from pain of the past is just a day-to-day reprieve. We must relentlessly pursue recovery on a daily basis. Those of us who have experienced chaos caused by our willful acts may have worshipped false gods such as drugs, sex, or money and may have participated in addictive relationships. For us, surrendering our lives to Christ can be the step that begins the process of leading us out of the mess that our lives had become.

Spiritual growth and development occur slowly and through discipline. The best example of the discipline of prayer is that of Jesus praying frequently to know his Father's will. He gave us his *Lord's Prayer* which is a foundation for our prayer life.

Lord's Prayer

Our Father, who art in heaven,
hallowed be thy Name,
thy kingdom come,
thy will be done,
on earth as it is in heaven.
Give us this day our daily bread.
And forgive us our trespasses,
as we forgive those
who trespass against us.
And lead us not into temptation,
but deliver us from evil.
For thine is the kingdom,
and the power, and the glory,
for ever and ever.
Amen.

In the *Lord's Prayer*, the most important element for recovery is "*Thy will be done, on earth as it is in heaven.*" This may be interpreted as "May your will be realized throughout all of space, time and creation. God, if it is to be done, it is for you to bring it about." As our self-esteem increases and Jesus Christ becomes a trusted friend, we grow more confident that he is with us even when we pray.

Praying for knowledge of God's will for us helps us set aside our self-serving motives and provides an opportunity for God to bestow his grace upon us in often surprising ways. We receive reassurance of God's presence and know that his will for us is to be restored to health.

An overview of prayer and meditation for a given day may be outlined as follows:

At the beginning of the day, review your plans.

— Ask God for direction in your thoughts and actions.

— Ask God to keep you free from self-pity, dishonesty, or selfishness.

— Ask for the guidance needed to take care of any problems.

— Ask God for freedom from self-will and be prepared to accept his solution.

— Avoid praying for something that might turn out to be harmful.

During the day, in moments of indecision or fear, ask God for inspiration and guidance.

— Become aware of the presence of the Holy Spirit and be willing to release your concern for a specific outcome.

— Pray to God as often as necessary during the day, asking him to remove the feeling, obsession, or addiction that is bothering you at the moment.

— Invite Jesus to be present with you in tense situations when you are facing temptations or personal confrontations.

— If possible, call a friend in recovery to identify and share what is happening.

At the end of the day, review the events that happened.

— Reflect about how willing you were to turn to God for courage and strength to handle the events of the day.

- Ask God for guidance in taking corrective action.
- Ask God for knowledge of his will for you.
- Ask God's forgiveness where needed and acknowledge that this review is not intended to cause obsessive guilt, worry, or remorse.
- Give thanks to God for the guidance and blessings that were part of the day.

Group Exercise

Refer to page 186 for *Week Three* meeting format.

- What does maturity in Christ mean to you? What specific steps do you wish to take to become more mature in Christ? _____

_____

_____

_____

_____

_____

_____

- Cite examples of your behavior that indicate you are immature. What steps can you take to correct this? _____

_____

_____

_____

_____

_____

_____

_____

- How does knowing the truth make you free? _____

_____

_____

_____

_____

_____

_____

- Cite an example when you prayed for knowledge of God's will. What was the outcome? _____

_____

_____

_____

_____

_____

_____

- Share a meaningful experience in using the journal as part of your recovery process. _____

_____

_____

_____

_____

_____

_____

_____

- What is your prayer request for yourself or others? _____

_____

_____

_____

Complete the following *Family Group Prayer Requests.*

_____ is praying for me.

I am praying for _____ and his/her prayer request is

_____

_____

_____

Chapter Four

Trusting Our Senses

. . . .

*B*eing reared in a dysfunctional home can deprive us of a true faith in God and a healthy understanding of the world around us. Many of us may not have been taught to trust our senses. As a consequence we have developed faulty perceptions and beliefs which need to be confronted and changed. Only then can the process of healing through Christ become real and ongoing.

From the moment we are born, we are being shaped and influenced by our senses. At first, our impressions of our surroundings are not clear. As time passes, we become increasingly focused on our environment—what we see, feel and touch. If we are frightened and our world is painful because of our parents' alcoholism, drug addiction, workaholism, or other dysfunction, our understanding and perspective of life can become warped and destructive.

We may grow up assuming that everyone lives like we do because we do not talk with others about what their lives are like. To us, others might appear well adjusted, and we may want to adopt their characteristics and behave as they do. However, something inside may keep nagging at us, trying to get our attention. Our inner voice may say, "Ask somebody. See if other people's lives are like this." But we seldom do, because we have been taught not to discuss such things.

There are various ways in which we respond to our environment. Some of us want to be good, follow the rules and avoid "rocking the boat." Others are less concerned with being good and behave in a disruptive manner that causes turmoil within the family. For many of us, isolating and withdrawing from the chaos of the family environment was our means of coping. These negative behaviors lay the groundwork for developing self-destructive tendencies in adulthood.

At some point, many of us realize that we don't like what we see in our home, but we still comply, adapt and seldom ask questions. We may be told that it's wrong to hit our brother, but we may see our father beat our mother. Our grandmother might tell us drinking alcohol is bad for us, but we watch our grandfather drink until he passes out. Mixed messages such as these can only result in pain, anger and confusion.

As we begin to look outside of our home more and more, we see people smiling and being polite, often saying one thing but doing another. Although this may feel uncomfortable to us, we usually keep hiding our pain and anger. Many of us draw the conclusion that we are the abnormal ones—that everyone else is normal.

Many of us adapt so well to our surroundings that we become insensitive to our feelings and begin to adjust to the behavior of those around us. We may even engage in those behaviors ourselves in order to escape our own reality. We might drink excessively, work too hard, or overeat. In many cases, we find that such behavior can numb our pain and distract us—if only for a short time.

As we fall further and further under the spell of self-destructive behavior, our understanding of God may become very distorted. It might be quite difficult for us to believe in a God who loves us and who wants the best for us, when the worst is happening to us. We may have trouble believing in the Lord at all because we can't understand how he could allow such pain.

We cannot know all of who God is—we can only get occasional glimpses. It is hard for anyone to understand why God permits suffering. But he has given us free will to behave as we desire, and he also gives us the promise that he will be present with us in our suffering. God gave us his son, Jesus, to help us understand part of who he is—to model ways of behavior for us and to die on the cross for us.

God appeared to us many times in the Bible in father images. If we have an earthly father who is abusive, absent, or dysfunctional in other ways, we may believe that God, our Heavenly Father, is just like our dad—totally unconcerned and wrapped up in his own little world. We may believe that God is absent, violent, or unfair. We might say to ourselves, "If God really cared, things would be different. If he really is in charge, why would all this be happening?"

As our doubts begin to increase, our view of God may become more distorted and cause us to reject standards of behavior that we know in our own heart to be right. It may be very difficult for us to find any evidence of God in our lives.

If we come from a dysfunctional home, our view of life needs adjusting. As our perception of reality is challenged, we may come to admit that what we have seen all along might not necessarily be accurate. Healing, recovery and maturity begin as we change our view of our environment. To correct our vision, we need a "new pair of glasses" with which to view the world and rid ourselves of our painful perspective.

If a loving, caring God was not introduced to us, we might not know of the Holy Spirit's healing power. Our perception of how we can be healed may be narrow. Through Christ this can be changed. In REVELATIONS 8:18 (NIV) Jesus said, "*I counsel you to buy from me...salve to put on your eyes, so you can see..*"

Healing and recovery become possible as we receive and accept Christ into our lives. When we accept God's unconditional love, our shame, emptiness and pain can be exposed safely, and our healing can begin.

Christ revealed to us that God is consistent, caring, present, understanding, concerned and faithful. When we choose to live in his radiance, he lights our path to recovery. In the light of his glory, we can finally begin to see and accept reality. As we draw closer to Christ, his arms are open wide to each of us.

We may start to admit to ourselves that God is not as unrealistic or unfair as we might have imagined. We learn that God is not unjust or angry all the time and accepts us the way we are. One of the most powerful experiences of all is to finally realize that God loves us even though we are imperfect. He wants us to realize our full potential and when we make the decision to change, he is there to help us if we let him.

As we start to recognize our potential for change, others will look different to us. Dad and mom may no longer seem so threatening. Our brothers and sisters may appear different. It may be easier to accept our spouse and children just as they are. Focusing our lives on Christ helps us see a new reality. *"Let us fix our eyes on Jesus, the author and perfecter of our faith..."* HEBREWS 12:2 (NIV). When we look to Christ more and more, our dysfunction can become function, our pain can turn to joy and our relationships can begin to work.

Dramatic change is possible with the help of the Holy Spirit. We can learn to thank God for our circumstances, instead of becoming discouraged and disillusioned. Rather than being disappointed in others, we may learn to see the reflection of Christ in them. And in looking through the eyes of Jesus, we can learn to experience delight, wonder and awe, instead of pain and despair.

The more we turn to Christ, the more possible it is for us to be changed from despair to glory. *"And we, who with unveiled faces all reflect the Lord's glory, are being transformed into his likeness with ever-increasing glory, which comes from the Lord, who is the Spirit."* 2 CORINTHIANS 3:18 (NIV). As our lives become more focused upon God, we start to look for godly male and female images. We search out healthy role models to mirror reflections of Christ for us and to show us how to live as functional adults.

Paul instructed us to look at the model of his life in order to know how to follow Christ and grow. *"Whatever you have learned or received or heard from me, or seen in me—put it into practice. And the God of peace will be with you."* PHILIPPIANS 4:9 (NIV). It is up to us to do as Paul instructed. We must stop focusing on the ungodly role models that are so pervasive in our society and focus on Christ, living in his light and truth.

Our ineffective behavior developed as we adapted to our chaotic environment. To the best of our ability we trusted our senses—often we guessed at how we were to behave and react in various situations. By participating in a Christ-centered recovery group, we learn to distinguish between behaviors that are self-destructive and those that are mutually supportive to ourselves and others. We also gain a better understanding of our thoughts and feelings. Learning new ways of relating often comes from what we discover as we share our lives with others who are also seeking wholeness through Christ's healing power.

Individual Exercise

● What mixed messages did you receive in your childhood home? ___

_____

_____

_____

_____

_____

_____

● In what ways did you adapt to the pain in your home of origin? ___

_____

_____

_____

_____

_____

_____

● How have you imitated the destructive actions you observed in your home? _____

_____

_____

_____

_____

_____

_____

- What misperceptions of healthy behavior and beliefs do you wish to change in your life now? _____

_____

_____

_____

_____

_____

- What did you do as a child to "keep peace" and not "rock the boat?" _

_____

_____

_____

_____

_____

_____

- What is your current view of God? _____

_____

_____

_____

_____

_____

_____

Recovery Tool: Personal Behavior Self-Examination

It is often easy for us to become sidetracked, especially when we have lived in denial, self-deception and delusion for much of our lives. We stay on track in our recovery by asking ourselves probing questions as well as praying for and receiving God's guidance.

This *Personal Behavior Self-Examination* is useful in keeping us on course and helping us to recognize when we are falling into old behavior patterns. The questions and related Bible passages are designed to help us look closely at our behavior toward God, ourselves and others. Answer these questions alone first and be honest with yourself. Then ask your friends in recovery what they perceive your answers might be and look honestly at any discrepancies between your answers and theirs. By performing this exercise, you can obtain some useful clues about progress you have made and behavior that needs changing.

Behavior toward God

"Surely you desire truth in the inner parts; you teach me wisdom in the inmost place." PSALM 51:6 (NIV).

- Give a recent example of how you asked God to help you express your thoughts and feelings freely. _____

_____

_____

_____

_____

"See to it that no one misses the grace of God and that no bitter root grows up to cause trouble and defile many." HEBREWS 12:15 (NIV).

- How do resentment and bitterness interfere with your relationship with God? _____

_____

_____

_____

_____

"I will say of the Lord, 'He is my refuge and my fortress, my God, in whom I trust.'" PSALM 91:2 (NIV).

- How are you learning to put your faith and trust in God? _____

  _____

  _____

  _____

  _____

  _____

"Trust in the Lord with all your heart and lean not on your own understanding; in all your ways acknowledge him, and he will make your paths straight." PROVERBS 3:5-6 (NIV).

- In what ways have you asked God to enable you to trust? _____

  _____

  _____

  _____

  _____

  _____

"I am the vine; you are the branches. If a man remains in me and I in him, he will bear much fruit; apart from me you can do nothing." JOHN 15:5 (NIV).

- How do you visualize God? _____

  _____

  _____

  _____

  _____

"Submit yourselves, then, to God. Resist the devil, and he will flee from you. Come near to God and he will come near to you. Wash your hands, you sinners, and purify your hearts, you double-minded." JAMES 4:7-8 (NIV).

- How have you started submitting to God in the healing process? ___

  _____

  _____

  _____

  _____

"That if you confess with your mouth, 'Jesus is Lord,' and believe in your heart that God raised him from the dead, you will be saved." ROMANS 10:9 (NIV).

- In what ways do you show your trust in Jesus Christ, your Lord and Savior? _____

_____

_____

_____

_____

Behavior toward yourself

"He is a double-minded man, unstable in all he does." JAMES 1:8 (NIV).

- What difficulty do you have in making decisions? _____

_____

_____

_____

"For by the grace given me I say to every one of you: Do not think of yourself more highly than you ought, but rather think of yourself with sober judgment, in accordance with the measure of faith God has given you." ROMANS 12:3 (NIV).

- What steps are you presently taking to achieve flexibility and balance in your life? _____

_____

_____

_____

_____

"There is no fear in love. But perfect love drives out fear, because fear has to do with punishment. The one who fears is not made perfect in love."
1 JOHN 4:18 (NIV).

- How does fear of rejection and failure affect your life? _____

_____

_____

_____

_____

"For if you forgive men when they sin against you, your heavenly Father will also forgive you. But if you do not forgive men their sins, your Father will not forgive your sins." MATTHEW 6:14-15 (NIV).

- What relationships cause anger and rage to build inside you? _____

  _____

  _____

  _____

  _____

- How are you dealing with compulsiveness, denial of feelings and helplessness? _____

  _____

  _____

  _____

  _____

Behavior toward others

"Simply let your 'Yes' be 'Yes,' and your 'No,' 'No'; anything beyond this comes from the evil one." MATTHEW 5:37 (NIV).

- How do you feel when you say "no" to people? _____

  _____

  _____

  _____

  _____

- How are the "don't talk," "don't trust" and "don't feel" rules affecting you now? _____

  _____

  _____

  _____

  _____

● What unhealthy family rules are still operating in your home life? _

_____

_____

_____

_____

"Do not judge, or you too will be judged. For in the same way you judge others, you will be judged, and with the measure you use, it will be measured to you."
MATTHEW 7:1-2 (NIV).

● How might your harsh and unforgiving judgments of others hinder your own recovery? _____

_____

_____

_____

_____

● How are you learning not to project blame onto other people? ____

_____

_____

_____

_____

Group Exercise

Refer to page 186 for the *Week Four* meeting format.

- What was your childhood image of God? _____

  _____

  _____

  _____

  _____

  _____

  _____

- What is your image of God now? _____

  _____

  _____

  _____

  _____

  _____

  _____

- List two painful or negative memories from your childhood. How are these memories affecting you today? _____

  _____

  _____

  _____

  _____

  _____

  _____

- List two pleasant or positive memories from your childhood. How are these memories affecting you today? _____

_____

_____

_____

_____

_____

- What is your major resentment toward another person? Describe how this resentment has negatively affected your life. _____

_____

_____

_____

_____

_____

_____

- What is your prayer request for yourself or others? _____

_____

_____

_____

_____

Complete the following *Family Group Prayer Requests.*

_____ is praying for me.

I am praying for _____ and his/her prayer request is

_____

_____

_____

Chapter Five

The Healing Touch

• • • • • • • • • • •

*B*eing adult children means that we are chronologically and biologically mature before we are emotionally mature. Most of us have some catching up to do in dealing with emotions, responsibilities and relationships. One of the ways we develop the ability to experience intimacy is through touching and being touched. Experiencing touch in a healthy way is a necessary part of our healing and crucial to our journey toward wholeness and maturity in Christ.

Because of poor role models in our home, we may be inadequately prepared for adult living. Negative influences were possibly more captivating to us than the men and women we knew who reflected Christ. During our formative years, we especially needed godly male and female models to learn what mature adults look and act like. If we are going to catch up in the areas in which we are deficient and properly prepare our own children for adult life, we need consistent and positive physical nurturing from healthy role models.

Many fathers in our society have opted out of family life, have taken out their anger on their wives and children or have in other ways shown their inadequacy as nurturers. Because of my own background and my relationship with my father, I believe it is particularly important that we have father role models who practice healthy, positive touching and nurturing.

Fathers can provide us with healthy images of God the Father by personal example. God-like role models can represent the values, morals and character of our Heavenly Father. By their attention, embrace, nurture, discipline, consistency and presence in our home, healthy fathers can show us those important aspects of God's nature.

We are created in the image and likeness of God, who has always interacted with his creation on a personal level. Although it may have seemed otherwise in our painful childhoods, God has never been absent, inattentive, or abusive. God showed us the importance of personal touch when he sent his only begotten Son to live with us. Touch was extremely important in Jesus' healing ministry, and today he touches us still.

Our being is confirmed as the Holy Spirit brings us forgiveness, healing, joy, encouragement, discipline and direction. When we invite Christ into our lives, his presence produces in us a sense of security, belonging and purpose. When we fail to respond to God's presence, we experience emptiness, fear and confusion. No matter what we do, God's offer is always open; he does not change in his desire and intent to touch our lives with great blessings.

If we are to become mature adults, it is important that we face any damages we may have sustained in the areas of intimate contact. Many of us who were raised in a dysfunctional home may not have experienced enough nurturing from our parents. We may have been either deprived of healthy intimacy or damaged by physical abuse.

Whatever our childhood difficulties were, we may be lacking in our abilities to give and receive closeness in a healthy way. Studies on early childhood development have consistently shown the importance of physical and verbal intimacy. Life is conceived and nurtured with intimate touch; it provides babies with the security necessary to begin proper physical, mental and emotional development.

Our earliest touch experiences create a life-long bond between our parents or primary caregivers and ourselves. From the time we are infants, we begin to express this need by asking for and desiring physical and verbal interaction. We develop a desire to stay close—to be rocked, to be held and talked to. We even show a need for a firm but loving touch to guide and discipline us.

As growing children, we continue to need nurturing, guidance and discipline. If we receive what we need, we will also learn to reach out and touch others.

Our need for touching and being touched continues throughout our pre-adolescent stage. The need for bonding, nurturing, caring, guidance and discipline remains constant through all the crucial stages of childhood development. During adolescence, we begin to desire more intimate contact while retaining all of our other needs for closeness. Our need for intimate touching is part of the exploration of our sexual identity which usually begins during puberty.

Sometime during puberty, most of us consciously or unconsciously begin the search for a mate—someone who can be our partner for life. This need for closeness may culminate in the formal commitment of marriage. Ideally, our sexual and intimate needs will be fulfilled with God's blessing in a marriage of whole, healthy partners.

Problems can occur if our needs at any stage of development are not met, or if they are met in the wrong way. Deprivation or physical abuse is devastating to the development of mature adult life. Following are some ways in which we may have experienced abuse or deprivation:

Nurturing
Lack of gentle, caressing strokes and holding in a loving manner.

Bonding
Lack of bonding due to unresponsive or absent parents or caregivers in our infancy or early childhood.

Affirmation and Acceptance
Lack of positive comments and gestures affirming our being, growth and accomplishments. Not being accepted for who we are, and having unrealistic expectations placed upon us.

Guidance
Absence of guidance and support in a loving and reassuring way.

Spirituality

Inadequate modeling or teaching about God's loving touch.

Discipline

Absence of loving, affirmative discipline. Use of excessive force that affects us physically and emotionally.

Physical Contact

Violence, such as venting anger physically.

Sexual Contact

Inappropriate touching in areas that cause sexual arousal in adults, sometimes leading to sexual intercourse.

Emotional Interaction

Continual criticism or blame, especially for events beyond our control. Unrealistic expectations that we fulfill adult emotional needs.

The results of negative touch experience or deprivation become most clear in our adult relationships, but usually start to become apparent in childhood. Any damage we may have suffered can affect us in many ways. Some of our behaviors that can be partially traced to abuse and deprivation are as follows:

— Fear of being touched.

— Withdrawal from close contact.

— Aloofness.

— Fear of intimacy.

— Problems expressing ourselves sexually as adults, even with a loving and caring partner.

— Sexual abuse of ourselves or others.

The prevalence of these symptoms in adults in our society is a clear indication that the incidence of touch abuse and deprivation is widespread. The sharp rise in the number of incidents involving violence, rape, incest, sexual abuse and mental illness prove that we are in danger.

Rather than being alarmed at the scope of the problem, we can trust that there is hope. Christ-centered recovery offers a powerful solution to this epidemic of abuse and deprivation. "*Just then a woman who had been subject to bleeding for twelve years came up behind him and touched the edge of his cloak. She said to herself, 'If I only touch his cloak, I will be healed.' Jesus turned and saw her. 'Take heart, daughter,' he said, 'your faith has healed you.' And the woman was healed from that moment.*" MATTHEW 9:20-22 (NIV). Jesus calls us to touch the hem of his garment—as this woman did—and be healed. We can be healed by Christ if we allow him to touch our deep wounds.

If we turn our healing over to God and trust the power of the Holy Spirit, there is hope for us. Some of the ways in which we may do this are:

— Ask Christ to come into our lives.

— Submit every area of our lives to God's loving guidance and control.

— Ask Christ to reveal and heal the areas of woundedness that continue to damage us.

— Stop blaming our parents or others who abused or deprived us.

— Refuse to let anyone touch us in an abusive or violent way.

— Learn the art of nurture in all our relationships.

— Give our mates and children the touch they need.

— Trust that God desires to touch our lives with nurture, affirmation, purpose and love.

— Becoming willing to receive forgiveness, cleansing, purity, joy, peace and power through the Holy Spirit.

If we have the courage to face our intimacy problems, we can greatly enhance our ability to move toward healing and wholeness through Christ. We can experience the joys of healthy and mature adult relationships.

Individual Exercise

● What were your childhood experiences of touch? _____

_____

_____

_____

_____

_____

_____

_____

In what ways do you feel abused by or deprived of touch now? _____

_____

_____

_____

_____

_____

_____

● How does Christ touch your life today? _____

_____

_____

_____

_____

_____

_____

_____

● As you are able, touch at least one person a day in an affirming way that feels comfortable to you. You might try a hug, a gentle touch, or a back rub. How do you feel about this idea? _____

_____

_____

_____

_____

_____

● Who was the male role model in your life that contributed most effectively to your well-being as a child? Describe your relationship with that person. _____

_____

_____

_____

_____

_____

● Who was the female role model in your life that contributed most effectively to your well-being as a child? Describe your relationship with that person. _____

_____

_____

_____

_____

_____

Recovery Tool: Scriptural Prescriptions

Healing and Christian maturity come through the practical application of Scripture to our lives and can be referred to as *Scriptural Prescriptions*. Some examples are:

"*Cast all your anxiety on him because he cares for you.*" 1 PETER 5:7 (NIV).
Anxiety attacks, burdens and concerns impair our growth and healing. At the end of each day we can identify the things that we are anxious or concerned about and ask God for guidance. As we proceed in recovery, we may find ourselves casting all cares on God as they arise. "Humble yourselves before the Lord, and he will lift you up." JAMES 4:10 (NIV).

It is true that God gives abundant grace to the humble. His grace is sufficient help for our natural weakness. Humility is not putting ourselves down. It is not demeaning or belittling ourselves. To humble ourselves is to gain and maintain God's perspective. "*For by the grace given me I say to every one of you: Do not think of yourself more highly* (or more lowly) *than you ought, but rather think of yourself with sober judgment, in accordance with the measure of faith God has given you.*" ROMANS 12:3 (NIV) (parentheses mine).

"*...whatever is true, whatever is noble, whatever is right, whatever is pure, whatever is lovely, whatever is admirable—if anything is excellent or praiseworthy—think about such things.*" PHILIPPIANS 4:8 (NIV).
Not only are we taught to think of ourselves from God's perspective, but we are also called by Scripture to think of the positive in all else. When we set our minds on the good and truth in others, we experience true peace and serenity. As part of learning to set our minds in tune with Scripture, we may want to set aside time to meditate on all that is lovely, fine and praiseworthy in God's creation.

These are a only few examples of how to use God's word as a personal prescription for growth and healing. Some find it helpful to read aloud positive affirmations from Scripture. Posting such an affirmation in a prominent place can help remind us of who and what we are as children of God. The more we are exposed to God's word, the more prepared we are for the touch of his healing grace. Following are some examples of Scriptural affirmations:

— Old things have passed away; all things have become new.

— I am kept by the power of God.

— I am complete in Jesus.

— I am sealed by the Holy Spirit of promise.

— Jesus Christ is my Lord, and I am a product of his love.

— I can do all things which strengthen me through Christ.

— Now, in the name of Jesus, I proclaim my liberty, freedom and peace through his love.

Remember that we are unique, unrepeatable miracles of God's grace in Christ. When we turn to him in all things, we allow his influence to change our thoughts, feelings and actions. As we apply God's word to our lives, we come to understand how he wishes us to live.

Group Exercise

Refer to page 186 for the *Week Five* meeting format.

- What behaviors do you see in yourself that result from earlier touch abuse or deprivation? _____

_____

_____

_____

_____

_____

_____

- What steps are you willing to take to bring more positive touch into your life? _____

_____

_____

_____

_____

_____

_____

- What areas of touch abuse or deprivation were most damaging to you as a child? How are they affecting your life today? _____

_____

_____

_____

_____

_____

_____

- Describe a recent situation that indicates you "cast all your anxiety on God." _____

  _____

  _____

  _____

  _____

  _____

- Share a meaningful experience in using the journal as part of your recovery process. _____

  _____

  _____

  _____

  _____

  _____

  _____

- What is your prayer request for yourself or others? _____

  _____

  _____

  _____

  Complete the following *Family Group Prayer Requests.*

  _____ is praying for me.

  I am praying for _____ and his/her prayer request is

  _____

  _____

  _____

Chapter Six

Becoming Childlike

. . . .

*O*nce again Jesus provides guidance for us. "...*'Who is the greatest in the Kingdom of Heaven?' He called a little child and had him stand among them. And He said, 'I tell you the truth, unless you change and become like little children, you will never enter the Kingdom of Heaven...'*" MATTHEW 18:1-3 (NIV).

As a result of our dysfunctional upbringing, many of us act childishly rather than childlike. The skills needed to help us mature were absent, and we developed behaviors that are immature. As part of our healing process, we need to learn how to be childlike by allowing ourselves to be playful. At the same time we need to be aware of our childishness and accept responsibility for ourselves.

Some examples of childish behavior are:

— Whining, manipulating or throwing temper tantrums to get our way.

— Thinking, talking and reasoning like a child.

— Demanding an excess of "toys" and creature comforts, or feeling we don't deserve to have such things.

— Not communicating our thoughts, feelings, or needs.

— Being unable to make or act on decisions.

— Letting other people think for us and care for us.

— Not facing the consequences of our behavior.

— Being self-centered, self-oriented and selfish.

— Not seeing ourselves as deserving positive attention.

— Pouting until others give in to our childish demands.

— Being timid and shy or rude and aggressive.

Paul said, "...*but when perfection* (maturity) *comes, the imperfect* (immature and childish) *disappears. When I was a child, I talked like a child, I thought like a child, I reasoned like a child. When I became a man, I put childish ways behind me. Now we see but a poor reflection as in a mirror; then we shall see face to face. Now I know in part; then I shall know fully, even as I am fully known.*" 1 CORINTHIANS 13:10-12 (NIV) (parentheses mine).

Childish behaviors we exhibit as adults cannot stop until we realize what we are doing and make an effort to change. Again, Christ can be our hope and example if we only let him. Scripture presents Christ as having been raised in a healthy, functional family system. From descriptions in the Bible, it seems that his parents did not live in reaction to one another; thus, he did not have to live in reaction to his parents. "*And Jesus increased in wisdom and stature, and in favor with God and man.*" LUKE 2:52 (KJV).

Jesus took full responsibility for all of his adult actions. There is no evidence in the Bible that indicates he developed the behavior patterns which are so often characteristic of adult children. Instead of blaming others, Jesus consistently forgave them. "*For if you forgive men when they sin against you, your Heavenly Father will also forgive you. But if you do not forgive men their sins, your Father will not forgive your sins.*" MATTHEW 6:14-15 (NIV). To be freed of dysfunction and thereby experience wholeness, it is important that we fully forgive and that we experience full forgiveness. Forgiving those who wounded us is an essential part of recovery.

To help us look at our own behavior, we can ask ourselves these questions:

— Do I look and act like an adult?

— Do I talk, think and reason like an adult?

— Do I make adult decisions?

— Do I carry out adult responsibilities?

— Do I take care of myself?

In searching for answers to these questions, it helps to reflect on situations or experiences from our past. Some of the following factors which contribute to childishness in adulthood may apply to our own childhood:

We may have been crushed in spirit by our parents.

"Fathers, do not exasperate your children; instead, bring them up in the training and instruction of the Lord" EPHESIANS 6:4 (NIV). *"A man's spirit sustains him in sickness, but a crushed spirit who can bear?"* PROVERBS 18:14 (NIV). A crushed spirit can result when we repeatedly experience broken promises, attacks on our self-worth or intentional neglect.

We may have been forced to grow up too fast.

When we have adult expectations and responsibilities placed on us as children, we often feel obligated to accomplish what was left undone by the adults in our lives. We might have been expected to fill in where they failed and understand life with adult comprehension. This may have kept us from the normal childhood experiences of playing, making mistakes and being spontaneous.

We may have had poor role models.

Adults who could be proper role models were often absent or didn't spend the time necessary to teach us. In many situations, we were expected to be adults instead of being allowed to be children. Because of this, we often come to hate the role of a mature adult. Many of us still equate any form of adulthood with painful and often embarrassing childhood memories.

We may have been punished abusively, often out of anger.

If we were punished for normal childhood misdeeds abusively and with anger, we were subjected to undue and unnecessary punishments. Many times we may have been condemned for simply being a child instead of being disciplined for willful disobedience. This form of punishment is very damaging and can be easily passed on to subsequent generations.

We may have been deprived of clearly defined rules or boundaries.

We might have been allowed to do what we thought was best in childhood, or we may have been made to follow crazy, nonsensical rules. In *Chapter Three*, we listed some of the crazy rules we might have grown up with such as "don't talk," "don't trust," "don't feel," and the damage that can come from obeying these rules. In order to function normally, we need clear instructions such as "You may watch television after you do your homework," or "I want to meet your friends before you go out with them."

Often, we either were not provided with the boundaries necessary in childhood, or our boundaries were unrealistic. For example, no one may have cared if we ever came home, or we may seldom have been allowed out of the house after school. Such treatment can result in a profound sense of insecurity and an inability to provide security for our own children.

Many problems which cause us to behave childishly can be a result of damage during crucial developmental periods of our lives. If we suffered deprivation or abuse during the first five years of our lives, we probably have difficulty trusting others and committing ourselves in a trusting relationship. It may be especially difficult for us to trust God, whom we cannot see. We can experience healing and learn to trust by allowing ourselves to receive healthy touch, nurturing and unconditional love from others.

If we suffered deprivation or abuse between the ages of five and nine, we may experience difficulties in reasoning, communication and understanding. We may lack the ability to express ourselves, our feelings and our goals, and our ability to think and act logically may be hindered.

If our curiosity was curtailed during this time, we may have problems speaking up for ourselves or believing we have something worthwhile to say. If we were not allowed to ask questions, or our questions went unanswered, we may feel unsure of our ability to make sound decisions.

Such problems can be healed in healthy relationships where we receive encouragement, patience and honest answers to our questions. To become whole, we need to communicate what we feel and think without fear of reprisal or rejection. It is also important to learn to ask the Holy Spirit for wisdom and discernment about how and what to communicate.

If our development was damaged during the ages of nine to fourteen, we may experience problems in relating to others. We may have difficulty in forming our own identity, feeling accepted for ourselves rather than for our performance, or doing what we honestly believe is best rather than what pleases others. If we were not affirmed for our person instead of our performance, our self-esteem is probably low, and our ability to handle peer pressure may be nonexistent.

Our healing can come through the acceptance and affirmation of our true selves in Christ. When we are appreciated for who we are instead of how we perform, we can begin to recover. When we find our identity, affirmation and acceptance in Christ and in our personal relationship with him, he extends his acceptance and affirmation of us through our family, friends and church community.

If we do not have godly, healthy role models between the ages of fifteen to twenty, we may very likely have trouble understanding and coping with our sexuality, careers, marriages and children. If our role models lived by double standards, we may lack a healthy belief system, godly values or positive convictions and character.

These four periods of development are crucial to our becoming functional adults. However, many of us are still living with an injured child inside of us instead of living in Christ. Part of putting away childish behavior is to honestly face our developmental dysfunctions and learn how to cope with life more effectively.

One of the ways we can heal in these areas is to seek out healthy role models, starting with Christ. *"For this very reason, make every effort to add to your faith goodness; and to goodness, knowledge; and to knowledge, self-control; and to self-control, perseverance; and to perseverance, godliness; and to godliness, brotherly kindness; and to brotherly kindness, love. For if you possess these qualities in increasing measure, they will keep you from being ineffective and unproductive..."* 2 PETER 1:5-9 (NIV).

Following are some of the healthy childlike qualities that we may want to incorporate into our adult lives:

— The ability to live an uncomplicated life by simplifying our schedules, priorities and goals.

— The ability to laugh, relax and play.

— The ability to be creative and fresh, rejoicing in the miracle of new life in everything we do.

— The ability to be flexible in the face of life's changes, without fear of the future.

— The ability to trust ourselves and others.

— The ability to have absolute faith and trust in God.

It is important that we determine what to retain from our childhood and what to give up. When we put away childish things and become childlike, we come into fullness and wholeness in Christ.

● List examples of your current childish behavior. _____

_____

_____

_____

_____

_____

_____

● What factors in your childhood contributed to your current childish behavior? _____

_____

_____

_____

_____

_____

_____

_____

● In what areas of your development were you forced to grow up too fast? _____

_____

_____

_____

_____

_____

_____

_____

● How can you find the acceptance and affirmation you need? _____

_____

_____

_____

_____

_____

_____

_____

● Describe your current ability to laugh, relax and play. _____

_____

_____

_____

_____

_____

_____

_____

● What childlike behaviors do you want to start practicing? _____

_____

_____

_____

_____

_____

_____

_____

Recovery Tool: Vital Passages

A creative way to use the Bible to aid in our recovery is to reflect on a vital passage and imagine ourselves as one of the main characters in the story other than Jesus. Pick a Bible passage that relates to ineffective behavior or to healing. Write at least two pages about the background leading up to the incident, how you felt during the incident, and how you feel after the incident. Following is an example of how this can be done:

One story describing dysfunctional behavior is that of Peter betraying Jesus after he was arrested. *"Simon, Simon, Satan has asked to sift you as wheat. But I have prayed for you, Simon, that your faith may fail. And when you have turned back, strengthen your brothers.' But he replied, 'Lord, I am ready to go with you to prison and to death.' Jesus answered, 'I tell you, Peter, before the rooster crows today, you will deny three times that you know me.'"* LUKE 22:31-34 (NIV).

"Then seizing him, they led him away and took him into the house of the high priest. Peter followed at a distance. But when they had kindled a fire in the middle of the courtyard and had sat down together, Peter sat down with them. A servant girl saw him seated there in the firelight. She looked closely at him and said, 'This man was with him.' But he denied it. 'Woman, I don't know him,' he said. A little later someone else saw him and said, 'You also are one of them.' 'Man, I am not!' Peter replied. About an hour later another asserted, 'Certainly this fellow was with him, for he is a Galilean.' Peter replied, 'Man, I don't know what you're talking about!' Just as he was speaking, the rooster crowed. The Lord turned and looked straight at Peter. Then Peter remembered the word the Lord had spoken to him: 'Before the rooster crows today, you will disown me three times.' And he went outside and wept bitterly." LUKE 22: 54-62 (NIV).

- How did you feel when Jesus said he had prayed that your faith would not fail and that you would strengthen your brothers? _____

_____

_____

_____

_____

_____

_____

- How did you feel when Jesus said you would betray him after you assured him you would go with him to prison and to death? _____

  _____

  _____

  _____

  _____

- How did you feel when people in the crowd after Jesus' arrest said they had seen you with him? _____

  _____

  _____

  _____

  _____

- What was going on in your mind when you denied him? _____

  _____

  _____

  _____

  _____

- What did it feel like when you looked at Jesus and suddenly remembered that he had predicted your betrayal? _____

  _____

  _____

  _____

  _____

A healing story is that of the bleeding woman. *"Just then a woman who had been subject to bleeding for twelve years came up behind him and touched the edge of his cloak. She said to herself, 'If I only touch his cloak, I will be healed.' Jesus turned and saw her. 'Take heart, daughter,' he said, 'your faith has healed you.' And the woman was healed from that moment."* MATTHEW 9:20-22 (NIV).

Imagine that you are the bleeding woman and that you go to a neighbor's house that you trust to tell her what happened.

● Describe how it felt to bleed for twelve years. _____

_____

_____

_____

● What had you heard about Jesus as a healer? _____

_____

_____

_____

● What gave you the courage to touch his cloak? _____

_____

_____

_____

● What did it feel like when Jesus spoke to you? _____

_____

_____

_____

_____

● How did it feel to be healed? _____

_____

_____

_____

_____

Group Exercise

Refer to page 186 for the *Week Six* meeting format.

● As a child, what were your boundaries? As an adult, how do you maintain healthy boundaries? _____

_____

_____

_____

_____

_____

_____

● Cite examples of your current behavior that indicate you are "becoming childlike." _____

_____

_____

_____

_____

_____

_____

● What difficulties do you have in relating to others? _____

_____

_____

_____

_____

_____

_____

- What difficulties do you have with trusting yourself and others? What do you believe causes this lack of trust? _____

  _____

  _____

  _____

  _____

  _____

  _____

- Who has sinned against you that you want to forgive? How will you accomplish this? _____

  _____

  _____

  _____

  _____

  _____

  _____

  _____

  _____

- What is your prayer request for yourself or others? _____

  _____

  _____

  _____

Complete the following *Family Group Prayer Requests.*

_____ is praying for me.

I am praying for _____ and his/her prayer request is

_____

_____

_____

Chapter Seven

Becoming Christ-Centered

• • • • • • • • • • •

*B*ecause we are adult children, some of us are totally wrapped up in ourselves and can only see life from a self-centered viewpoint. Everything revolves around us. "I want, I feel, I believe, I need" often dominate our conversation. Focusing on our own problems sometimes becomes an obsession. Or, we may behave in the opposite manner and become totally self-effacing, obsessed with others' problems and seldom considering our own difficulties. Neither of these extremes will lead to wholeness and healing, nor will they initiate and support healthy relationships.

In either case, the insanity of our parental home often drives us to prove ourselves to others. Our need to excel in all that we do causes us to focus on our performance rather than accepting that we are worthy just as we are. Some of us may lose sight of our true selves through fear, self-delusion, or fantasy. Ultimately, we may become self-centered. Many of us were not taught that we were created by God and made in his image and likeness. "*And God saw every thing that he had made, and, behold, it was very good...*" GENESIS 1:31 (KJV).

God made everything—oceans, mountains, seasons, animals and people—to be unique and different. We are all individual miracles of God's creativity. "*For you created my inmost being; you knit me together in my mother's* womb. *I praise you because I am fearfully and wonderfully made; your works are wonderful, I know that full well. My frame was not hidden from you when I was made in the secret place. When I was woven together in the depths of earth, your eyes saw my unformed body; All the days ordained for me were written in your book before one of them came to be.*" PSALM 139:13-16 (NIV).

Instead of understanding that we are cherished, we may have been led to believe that we were unwanted. Perhaps we felt fortunate even to have been born, although in times of great pain we may not feel grateful. Our ability to accept ourselves as we are, and as God intends us to be, was hindered during these early days of trauma, rejection and abandonment. Thus, it is not surprising that our self-identity became distorted.

Often, members of a pain-inflicting family system suffer severe abuse. Such mistreatment can be physical, verbal, sexual, or emotional, and each of these forms of attack harms us in various ways. Verbal abuse can damage our self-esteem and physical abuse can threaten our very lives. Sexual abuse makes it difficult for us to have healthy relationships, whereas emotional abuse can inhibit our ability to cope with even the normal trials of life. Any harassment we may have suffered from others can cause us to become self-centered as a defense against pain.

Having experienced abuse as children, we sometimes set ourselves up to harm our own bodies with self-destructive, unloving and life-threatening behavior. If we were molested by our parents or caretakers, we may have trouble understanding the sacred nature of our bodies or believing they were created to be a dwelling place for God.

Sexual abuse can be especially damaging to our emotional and spiritual development. The Bible teaches us that sexual immorality or impurity can cause us to sin against our own body. "...*The body is not meant for sexual immorality, but for the Lord, and the Lord for the body...All other sins a man commits are outside his body, but he who sins sexually sins against his own body. Do you not know that your body is a temple of the Holy Spirit, who is in you, whom you have received from God? You are not your own; you were bought at a price. Therefore honor God with your body.*" 1 CORINTHIANS 6:13,18-20 (NIV).

Another problem that can give rise to self-centeredness is the pride, deception and striving that can become so deeply rooted in our lives when we are raised in a dysfunctional home. Illustrations of this can be found in three stories of Jacob and Esau in the book of Genesis, chapters 25-36. Isaac's wife, Rebekah, gave birth to twin sons, Esau and Jacob. Esau was born first and, therefore, was entitled to his father's birthright and inheritance. Isaac favored Esau and Rebekah was partial to Jacob.

The first story tells of the day Esau came in famished, and Jacob refused to give him food until Esau sold him his birthright. We can clearly see Jacob's deception as he conned his elder brother Esau out of his birthright.

The second story happened when Isaac was old and his eyes weak. Rebekah persuaded Jacob to pretend he was Esau and take food to Isaac to receive the blessing Isaac had promised Esau. We watch Jacob follow his mother Rebekah's plan of deception to gain his father Isaac's blessing. Rebekah modeled and taught Jacob to deceive, lie and con in order to get what she wanted from her husband, Isaac. Meanwhile she pretended that she was doing all this for her child.

The third story comes many years later when Jacob and his tribes were preparing to meet Esau and his tribes. Jacob wanted to greet Esau warmly and give him many gifts but was afraid of how his brother would react to him. While waiting for Esau to arrive, Jacob wrestled with a man and wrenched his hip which caused him to limp. Jacob would not let the man depart until the man blessed him. After Jacob told the man his name, the man said "...*your name will no longer be Jacob, but Israel, because you have struggled with God and with men and have overcome.*" GENESIS 32:28 (NIV). The man would not tell Jacob his name but blessed him before he left. Jacob said, "...*I saw God face to face, and yet my life was spared.*" GENESIS 32:30 (NIV). The reunion of the brothers took place with love, generosity and forgiveness on both sides. Jacob's lifestyle of deception and estrangement from his brother was finally ended and healed by wrestling with God.

Jacob's stories can help us learn about our own lives. Our parents may have used us as pawns in their manipulative games, much like Rebekah used Jacob. We may have learned to lie, deceive and con to please someone else, as Jacob did. Like Esau, we often sell our birthrights and harbor bitterness, revenge and other violence in our hearts. Like Jacob, we might have to go through years of suffering the consequences of our selfish behavior before we ever get to the point of surrender to God. We may need to wrestle with God and become handicapped like Jacob did before we learn that we can no longer play God and that we need to turn over our brokenness to him before we can be healed.

When our self-image is damaged, we may develop certain characteristics, beliefs and behaviors in an effort to protect ourselves from the harsh realities of our lives. As a result of our low self-image, we may become one or more of the following:

Self-centered

Acting as though we believe the world revolves around us.

Self-righteous

Wanting to always be right and constantly trying to justify our actions.

Self-deluded

Not seeing ourselves and our lives realistically; rather, concocting fantasies that we begin to believe and act upon.

Self-deceptive

Wearing facades or masks in an attempt to cover up our true state of being. Constantly denying our true feelings, reactions, or motives.

Selfish

Concentrating on our own advantage, pleasure, or well-being without regard for others.

Prideful

Acting as though we believe we are better than everyone else.

Arrogant

Behaving as though we are the only one who knows what is best for us and for our families. Convincing ourselves we can be healed without help from God or anyone else.

Self-destructive

Indulging in life-threatening behaviors which can destroy us mentally, physically, emotionally and spiritually.

Any or all of these conditions can keep us from finding our true selves in Christ. If we are to be all that we were created to be, there is a journey to self-discovery awaiting us; and, if we let him, Christ will be our guide.

Whether we want to believe it or not, we were created in the image and likeness of God, and God wants us to fulfill the potential he created in each of us. This image is our true self, deep within, submerged inside our wounded child and striving to be liberated. When we allow the child within to be healed and liberated by the loving touch of the Holy Spirit, we can begin to discover who we were created to be.

God has blessed each of us with worth, uniqueness, gifts, talents, personality, vocation and purpose. Our birthright, inheritance and identity were purchased by the death of his only Son, our Lord Jesus Christ. This realization can certainly have a positive impact on our self-image and can help us greatly in our recovery.

As we turn from our dysfunctional, damaged selves and become the person God created us to be, we can begin to put our faith in Christ, rather than in ourselves. We can begin to see who we are in Christ, rather than who we are apart from him. We can come to know that it is through the Holy Spirit that we can realize our full potential.

In transforming ourselves into Christ-centered beings, we go through a metamorphosis from self-orientation to Christ-orientation. *"Therefore, if anyone is in Christ, he is a new creation; the old has gone, the new has come!"* 2 CORINTHIANS 5:17 (NIV). During this process, we undergo numerous changes, much like the transformation of a caterpillar to a butterfly. Our lives become less self-centered as we leave the pain of our past behind us and gradually learn to put more of our trust in God.

There are some major changes that occur in our behavior when we undergo a metamorphosis as the Holy Spirit works in us:

We learn to stop playing God and submit our lives to Christ.

We realize that surrendering to Christ is more effective than playing God. *"...if you confess with your mouth, 'Jesus is Lord,' and believe in your heart that God raised him from the dead, you will be saved. For it is with your heart that you believe and are justified, and it is with your mouth that you confess and are saved. As the Scripture says, 'Anyone who trusts in him will never be put to shame.'"* ROMANS 10: 9-11 (NIV).

We exchange our preoccupation with self for a life in Christ.

We no longer put our main emphasis on ourselves. *"I have been crucified with Christ and I no longer live, but Christ lives in me. The life I live in the body, I live by faith in the Son of God, who loved me and gave himself for me."* GALATIANS 2:20 (NIV).

We nurture our new true self by examining ourselves in the light of God's word.

"Examine yourselves to see whether you are in the faith; test yourselves. Do you not realize that Christ Jesus is in you...For we cannot do anything against the truth, but only for the truth. We are glad whenever we are weak, but you are strong; and our prayer is for your perfection..." 2 CORINTHIANS 13:5, 8-9 (NIV). *"My grace is sufficient for you, for my power is made perfect in weakness..."* 2 CORINTHIANS 12:9 (NIV). Christ shows his strength through us when we are willing to depend on him. *"But grow in the grace and knowledge of our Lord and Savior Jesus Christ..."* 2 PETER 3:18 (NIV).

We live our new lives in service to God.

Our body can now become a vessel for God to use as he chooses. Through our new self, our true self in Christ, we can express our values, gifts and calling. *"Through Jesus, therefore, let us continually offer to God a sacrifice of praise—the fruit of lips that confess his name. And do not forget to do good and share with others, for with such sacrifices God is pleased."* HEBREWS 13:15-16 (NIV). Our new life is marked with sacrificial living, praise, worship and service to others.

In our new true self, there is a new hunger.

We no longer strive for acceptance; instead, we desire constantly to please our Heavenly Father. As we become Christ-centered, we cease striving fruitlessly for perfection and become content with who we were made to be. Our new self becomes fulfilled as the Holy Spirit works in us, and we are more able to appreciate the beauty of God's great gift of life. *"Therefore, I urge you, brothers, in view of God's mercy, to offer your bodies as living sacrifices, holy and pleasing to God—this is your spiritual act of worship. Do not conform any longer to the pattern of this world, but be transformed by the renewing of your mind. Then you will be able to test and approve what God's will is—his good, pleasing and perfect will. For by the grace given me I say to everyone of you: Do not think of yourself more highly than you ought, but rather think of yourself with sober judgment, in accordance with the measure of faith God has given you."* ROMANS 12:1-3 (NIV).

● List the distortions you see in your self-image. _____

_____

_____

_____

_____

_____

_____

● Describe situations which demonstrate that you are self-centered.
   What can you do to correct this? _____

_____

_____

_____

_____

_____

_____

● What obstacles do you see in your own behavior that keep you from
   becoming more Christ-like? _____

_____

_____

_____

_____

_____

_____

- How can you nurture yourself by living in the light of God's word?

  _____

  _____

  _____

  _____

  _____

  _____

  _____

  _____

- Cite examples that indicate you are becoming Christ-centered. _____

  _____

  _____

  _____

  _____

  _____

  _____

  _____

- What was special for you on this day? _____

  _____

  _____

  _____

  _____

  _____

  _____

  _____

Recovery Tool: Making Amends

The following material, adapted from *The Twelve Steps—A Spiritual Journey*, can help us understand the importance of making amends to those we have hurt by our dysfunctional behavior.

Being willing to make amends improves our relationships with ourselves and others and leads us out of isolation and loneliness. As we continue to welcome Christ's presence into our hearts, we can develop a new openness with others that prepares us for the face-to-face admission of our past misconduct. With this tool, we examine each past misdeed and identify those involved. Our intention is to make amends in order to heal our past so that God can transform the present.

As Christians, we are taught the importance of having and maintaining deep, loving relationships. Through Christ's example, we see how he devoted his ministry to loving people and encouraging them to love one another. Jesus taught us that being reconciled to God requires reconciliation with other human beings. In this process, we prepare ourselves to carry out God's master plan for our lives by becoming willing to make amends. Once we have prepared our list of those whom we have harmed, we are able to extend our love and acceptance not only to the injured persons, but to all members of God's family.

When thinking about persons we have harmed, we see how our behavior has played a major part in sabotaging our lives and our relationships. The following behaviors are typical for adult children and are seen in many of us. Describe a recent situation when you behaved this way, or describe a situation showing the progress you have made in this area. If this behavior is not an issue for you, note that. Discuss your responses with friends in recovery to see how they perceive your behavior in these areas.

- When we become angry, we often harm ourselves more than others. This may result in feelings of depression or self-pity. _____

_____

_____

_____

- Persistent financial problems resulting from our irresponsible actions cause difficulty with our family and creditors. _____

_____

_____

_____

- When confronted with an issue about which we feel guilty, we lash out at others rather than looking honestly at ourselves. _____

_____

_____

_____

- Frustrated by our lack of control, we behave aggressively and intimidate those around us. _____

_____

_____

_____

- Because of our indiscriminate sexual behavior, true intimacy is impossible to achieve or maintain. _____

_____

_____

_____

- Our fear of abandonment sometimes destroys our relationships, because we do not allow others to be themselves. We create dependency and try to control another's behavior in an effort to maintain the relationship as we want it to be. _____

_____

_____

_____

- While trying to fulfill our unmet needs, we often become obsessive or compulsive. _____

    _____

    _____

    _____

    _____

- When we feel uneasy around other people, we often tend to isolate ourselves. _____

    _____

    _____

    _____

    _____

- We often compare ourselves to others and feel inferior. _____

    _____

    _____

    _____

    _____

- Afraid to take emotional risks, we often withhold our feelings, are uncommunicative or give in to others' wants and needs. _____

    _____

    _____

    _____

    _____

Group Exercise

Refer to page 186 for the *Week Seven* meeting format.

- Describe what you consider to be your outer, apparent self. _____

  _____

  _____

  _____

  _____

  _____

  _____

- Describe what you consider to be your inner, true self. _____

  _____

  _____

  _____

  _____

  _____

  _____

  _____

- Describe your uniqueness, gifts and calling in Christ. _____

  _____

  _____

  _____

  _____

  _____

  _____

  _____

● What does "making amends" mean to you? _____
_____
_____
_____
_____
_____
_____
_____

● Share a meaningful experience in using the journal as part of your recovery process. _____
_____
_____
_____
_____
_____
_____
_____

● What is your prayer request for yourself or others? _____
_____
_____
_____
_____

Complete the following *Family Group Prayer Requests.*

_____ is praying for me.

I am praying for _____ and his/her prayer request is
_____
_____
_____

Chapter Eight

Becoming an Adult

. . . .

*B*ecoming more aware of our condition as adult children helps us realize that healing is necessary if we are going to grow up and become functional adults. As we begin to change the internal structure of our lives, external changes will also occur. As Christians, we know that the Holy Spirit can assist us in making these changes. We need only to be willing to receive his help and that of our brothers and sisters in Christ.

We have already looked at possible areas where our woundedness needs healing. We might realize that we lack healthy role models or need to view life from Christ's perspective instead of our own. We may want to recover from touch abuse and deprivation or let go of childish and self-centered behavior. As we come to see and touch Jesus personally, our lives begin to reflect the grace of his healing love. It is a revelation to understand that God actually wants us to be whole! He wants us to experience wholeness and wants to help us change our inner structure.

The idea of finding healing through Christ might be hard to comprehend for those of us who are still licking the emotional wounds of our childhood. It may seem too good to be true, for many of us have adjusted to lives filled with hurt. For some of us, pain has become normal; others may be numb to the reality of our suffering.

In an attempt to protect ourselves from pain, we may have built a wall of denial around ourselves. Through our denial, we are able to pretend that things aren't as bad as they seem or that our imagination is just too active. Because we were hurt too much as children, we decided long ago to either ignore our pain or to deny it until it stopped.

As hard as we try to hide our discomfort and appear normal, others often notice that something is wrong with us. Perhaps they tell us we aren't in touch with our feelings or that we don't realize the extent of our destructive behavior. We may be accused of reacting too strongly, making a big deal out of normal pressures or being too inflexible. We might hear that we always appear sad, depressed and negative. Our families may tell us that we seem happy and content in public but behave differently in private. We could be accused of being distant, uncaring and incapable of close or intimate relationships. Or we might hear that we smother those close to us. People who live and work with us may tell us they feel like hostages. They may see us as making crazy demands, saying one thing and meaning another. Perhaps we hear that we act as though we are being driven by something inside—that we don't ever seem to relax, laugh, or have fun.

However painful it is to hear such statements from those close to us, we need to listen to what they are saying. Frequently, it is those who are closest to us who can most clearly evaluate our behavior for what it really is. Their advantage is that they are not surrounded by a wall of denial like we are. To the degree that we are willing, hearing their views can help us make the important changes necessary for our healing.

Our denial, projection, defense mechanisms and self-deception need to be broken through before true healing can occur. As damaged adults, we require a great deal of loving ministry to get us to the point of being treatable. By participating in a Christ-centered recovery group, listening to each other and praying together, we can slowly break through our defenses and move through healing to wholeness.

It is important that we accept the responsibility for our present condition and the problems it has caused us and others. Healing and maturity deepen as we take charge of our lives. We can't excuse our behavior by projecting the blame for it outside of ourselves and onto others. We need to see that many of our present problems result from past painful situations over which we had no control. However, accepting and acknowledging these occurrences is only part of the process. We need to take responsibility for ourselves, then share our insights with others in Christ-centered recovery, as well as with God in prayer.

Jesus tells us, *"Then you will know the truth, and the truth will set you free."* JOHN 8:32 (NIV). We may wonder what the truth really is. We can trust that whatever God says is factual, especially what he says about us. Sometimes he even uses those around us to help us recognize reality. Jesus also tells us, *"Sanctify them by the truth, your word is truth."* JOHN 17:17 (NIV). God's truth may not necessarily be consistent with our present perceptions, but as we learn to trust in the outcome, we begin to see that it is often our perceptions that are incorrect.

When we are accountable for our own actions and stop defending ourselves or projecting responsibility onto others, we are in a position to receive forgiveness, cleansing and healing. That is the real truth that God reveals to us. Our reactions of bitterness, judgment, anger, resentment and hate are created by us and belong to us, not to others. We cannot excuse our behavior, we can only alter it. We *"...are without excuse."* ROMANS 1:20 (NIV).

Our parents do not stand in our place before God—we do. We have no justification for our dysfunction as we stand before Christ. We are judged by our own behavior, and God is principally concerned with our words, thoughts, attitudes, habits and actions. We answer for all that we have thought and done, not for what someone else did or did not do. We can be grateful that we stand before the same Christ who shed his healing blood for us. *"But God demonstrates his own love for us in this: While we were still sinners, Christ died for us."* ROMANS 5:8 (NIV).

As part of becoming healthy adults, we need to realize and accept our present condition as adult children. Isaiah gives an apt description of us in the midst of our dysfunction, pain and reaction to our past, *"...makes the heart of this people calloused; makes their ears dull and closes their eyes. Otherwise, they may see with their eyes, hear with their ears, understand with their hearts, and turn and be healed."* ISAIAH 6:10 (NIV). *"Why should you be beaten anymore? Why do you persist in rebellion? Your whole head is injured, your whole heart afflicted. From the sole of your foot to the top of your head there is no soundness—only wounds and welts and open sores, not cleansed or bandaged or soothed with oil."* ISAIAH 1:5-6 (NIV). Admitting that we are in a similar condition can be a big step toward our healing.

Rather than rebelling against God, it helps to trust that he can and does understand our predicament. He knows better than we do that ours is a delicate condition and does not blame us. God does not in any way assault or abuse us. *"...For the Lord comforts his people and will have compassion on his afflicted ones."* ISAIAH 49:13 (NIV). *"Surely he took up our infirmities and carried our sorrows...he was pierced for our transgressions, he was crushed for our iniquities...and by his wounds we are healed."* ISAIAH 53:4-5 (NIV).

God does not forget us or abandon us even when our lives seem bleak. He *"...plans to prosper you and not to harm you, plans to give you a hope and a future."* JEREMIAH 29:11 (NIV). God loves us so much that he sent his son Jesus to minister to us—to show us his compassion and concern. Jesus quoted the prophet Isaiah to help explain his purpose here on earth. *"The Spirit of the Lord is on me, because he has anointed me to preach good news to the poor. He has sent me to proclaim freedom for the prisoners and recovery of sight for the blind, to release the oppressed, to proclaim the year of the Lord's favor."* LUKE 4:18-19 (NIV).

God alone can right the wrong done to us. If we open ourselves to him, his Holy Spirit can heal our grief and pain. The Holy Spirit comforts those who mourn the losses of a painful childhood and brings to maturity those who did not receive an adequate foundation for adult life.

It is God's will that we become whole. Our responsibility is to face our pain, be responsible for ourselves, admit to our rebellious behavior and accept the offer of Christ's healing. When we are able to fulfill these requirements, we will be able to live a functional life. *"But if we walk in the light, as he is in the light, we have fellowship with one another, and the blood of Jesus, his Son, purifies us from all sin."* I JOHN 1:7 (NIV).

We can gauge our progress by the degree to which we are becoming transparent. As we continue to break out of our denial and allow ourselves to be vulnerable, we can receive and enjoy continuous healing. We become aware of our feelings and begin to learn how to be our true selves with others. As we face our truths and live in the light of our reality, we become real to others as well as to ourselves.

As we live in the light of God's warmth and truth, we awaken to the reality of his love for us. We come to see that God really does love us because we are lovable. For many of us this is in stark contrast to the environment of rejection and disapproval in our dysfunctional family system where we learned that we are not worth loving.

In our pain and confusion we may have judged the love of God by negative experiences, rather than by what God has said and done. We may also judge his love and intentions towards us by what others have or have not done. Even though both of these judgments may be understandable in the light of how we were raised, they could not be farther from the truth. *"God demonstrated his love towards us, in that while we were yet sinners, Christ died for us."* ROMANS 5:8 (KJV). *"For God so loved the world that he gave his one and only Son..."* JOHN 3:16 (NIV). It is so freeing when we come to know that God's love for us is real—that he will never fail us. We cannot exhaust or frustrate his love. Whether we are functional or dysfunctional, God still loves us.

To stay on the road to our ultimate destination toward healing and wholeness, we must learn to recognize and receive God's love. In Paul's prayer for the Ephesian believers, he speaks to us as well. *"...And I pray that you, being rooted and established in love, may have power, together with all the saints, to grasp how wide and long and high and deep is the love of Christ, and to know this love that surpasses knowledge—that you may be filled to the measure of all the fullness of God."* EPHESIANS 3:17-19 (NIV).

If we are going to attain wholeness and health, it will be because we are convinced of the immense power of Christ's love for us. This devotion is evidence that healing is real and possible. We need God's love for our own growth and nurture just as a flower needs the sun, rain and nutrients from the soil for its blooming.

In addition to becoming convinced of God's love, we need to recognize the presence of his grace in our lives. God showers his grace upon us, even in the bleakest times. We need only be open to recognize and receive it. Even though we may be severely damaged, God's grace is sufficient to heal all our weakness and woundedness. *"...Continue to work out your salvation* (health and wholeness) *with fear and trembling* (with awe of God's healing grace and love, and respect for God's timing and purpose), *for it is God who* works in you to will and to act according to his good purpose." PHILIPPIANS 2:12-13 (NIV) (parentheses mine).

Now let's look at the **Prayer of St. Francis** as a tool to aid us in applying these healing truths to our lives and to the lives of others. St. Francis of Assisi spent his later life among adults in pain, showing them how to find healing by trusting in the Lord. His prayer provides us with an overview of biblical ministry. He prayed:

"Lord, make me an instrument of thy peace "

To receive or minister healing, it is important to first address Christ as Lord of our lives. It is only as we submit to our Lord that we function as Christ intends. St. Francis proclaimed that being an instrument of God's peace is primary to our healing. He understood that when we turn our lives over to God, we experience great peace of mind. *"And the peace of God, which transcends all understanding, will guard your hearts and your minds in Christ Jesus."* PHILIPPIANS 4:7 (NIV). *"Thou wilt keep him in perfect peace, whose mind is stayed on thee, because he trusteth in thee".* ISAIAH 26:3 (KJV). In the Sermon on the Mount Jesus says, *"blessed are the peacemakers."* MATTHEW 5:9 (NIV).

"Where there is hatred, let me sow love "

To prepare ourselves for sowing love, we ask whether we truly love others or whether there is anyone toward whom we have resentment. It can be a very profound experience to release our negative feelings and pray for someone we resent. We soften our harsh feelings when we become channels for God's love to flow to his children.

We can sow love by extending a sense of security to others. *"Love is patient, love is kind. It does not envy, it does not boast, it is not proud. It is not rude, it is not self-seeking, it is not easily angered, it keeps no record of wrongs. Love does not delight in evil but rejoices with the truth. It always protects, always trusts, always hopes, always perseveres. Love never fails..."* 1 CORINTHIANS 13:4-8 (NIV).

Love doesn't allow us to abuse, take advantage of, or try to control others. It is vitalized by actions of kindness. Love defends another's highest good and doesn't have to claim rights; it seeks to behave or act right. Love makes us servants and givers of encouragement, affirmation and support to all. It makes us feel like we belong and have purpose. Love does not fear rejection, therefore it enables us to share and be real with others.

"Where there is injury, pardon "

There is much injury in a dysfunctional family that needs pardoning. We must be aware that true forgiveness is necessary before there can be permanent healing. Jesus showed us how forgiving he expects us to be: *"Then Peter came to Jesus and asked, 'Lord, how many times shall I forgive my brother when he sins against me? Up to seven times?' Jesus answered, 'I tell you, not seven times, but seventy-seven times.'"* MATTHEW 18:21-22 (NIV). Christ pardons us and empowers us to forgive others. It is wonderfully healing to give and receive forgiveness in all our relationships—with God, ourselves and others.

"Where there is doubt, faith "

To restore faith into our lives, we need to remove any doubts we have developed. Skepticism can keep us locked into our woundedness, because it prevents us from trusting ourselves and others. When we doubt God, we are implying that God is neither willing nor able to heal us.

Faith, through Christ, is as real as the doubts that plagued our lives before recovery. *"Now faith is being sure of what we hope for and certain of what we do not see."* HEBREWS 11:1 (NIV). Faith enables us to be free from the pain and suspicion that resulted from being betrayed as a child. *"I consider that our present sufferings are not worth comparing with the glory that will be revealed in us."* ROMANS 8:18 (NIV).

ROMANS 10:17 (NIV) tells us: *"Consequently, faith comes from hearing the message and the message is heard through the word of Christ."* Our faith can be formed by being attentive to the Holy Spirit and seeing him at work in our lives, as well as in the lives of others. Jesus said, *"I have told you these things, so that in me you might have peace. In this world you will have trouble, but take heart! I have overcome the world."* JOHN 16:33 (NIV).

"Where there is despair, hope "

The sense of hopelessness and the pervasive depression that is so prevalent in the lives of many adult children is dispelled in Christ. *"And hope does not disappoint us, because God has poured out his love into our hearts by the Holy Spirit, whom he has given us."* ROMANS 5:5 (NIV). Hope, poured into our hearts by the Holy Spirit, empowers us to overcome the despair we encounter and frees us to continue on our journey to recovery. Paul stated, *"And now these three remain: faith, hope and love."* 1 CORINTHIANS 13:13 (NIV). In

Christ, our hope of having a functional life can be fulfilled as we learn to trust God's promise of healing to wholeness.

"Where there is darkness, light "

Any Christ-centered recovery strategy involves moving from a life lived in darkness to a life flooded with the light of Christ. If we do not face the darkness in our lives, our recovery can be retarded. St. Francis realized the importance of illuminating the shadows of our existence which only precipitates further pain and confusion. "*Now the Lord is the Spirit, and where the Spirit of the Lord is, there is freedom. And we, who with unveiled faces all reflect the Lord's glory, are being transformed into his likeness with ever-increasing glory, which comes from the Lord, who is the Spirit.*" 2 CORINTHIANS 3:17-18 (NIV).

"Where there is sadness, joy "

St. Francis knew the joy that is a part of healing. When we are filled with the Holy Spirit, our sadness turns to pleasure. "*...Instead, be filled with the Spirit. Speak to one another with psalms, hymns and spiritual songs. Sing and make music in your heart to the Lord, always giving thanks to God the Father for everything, in the name of our Lord Jesus Christ.*" EPHESIANS 5:18-20 (NIV).

As we become whole, we begin to draw from a new well deep within our souls. "*...but whoever drinks the water I give him will never thirst. Indeed, the water I give him will become in him a spring of water welling up to eternal life.*" JOHN 4:14 (NIV). With Christ in our hearts, there is literally a well of joy overflowing in our lives. "*...You will fill us with joy in your presence...*" PSALM 16:11 (NIV). Our depression, anger, fear, resentment and self-pity can become transformed by the jubilation of the Lord. "*...the joy of the Lord is your strength.*" NEHEMIAH 8:10 (NIV). In working closely with God, we can let go of our childhood pain and walk in the joy of his presence.

> *"O, Divine Master, grant that I may not so much seek to be consoled as to console; to be understood as to understand; to be loved as to love; for it is in giving that we receive; it is in pardoning that we are pardoned; and it is in dying that we are born to eternal life."*

An attitude of humility facilitates our healing. Disciples James and Peter tell us that God gives grace to the humble. By that they do not refer to false humility, denying our gifts and uniqueness, but a true humbling of ourselves in service to others in the name of Christ. This healthy attitude which helps us to console, understand, love and pardon is reflective of Christ's attitude. "*Do nothing out of selfish ambition or vain conceit, but in humility consider others better than yourselves. Each of you should look not only to your own interests, but also to the interests of others. Your attitude should be the same as that of Christ Jesus.*" PHILIPPIANS 2:3-5 (NIV).

As we work to restructure our lives, we uncover special areas that need healing prayer. A prayer such as the **Prayer of St. Francis** can be applied systematically to the areas of our lives that are still wounded. Such areas include the following:

Grief and a sense of loss

Most of us need the healing power of Christ in this area because of the great losses we have suffered. Missing out on a normal childhood, being deprived of intimate and healthy relationships and lacking of proper training in developing adult skills are but a few of the losses that most adult children have experienced.

Healing requires us to face our misfortunes and grieve them, for he came "*...to comfort all who mourn, and provide for those who grieve...to bestow on them a crown of beauty instead of ashes, the oil of gladness instead of mourning, and a garment of praise instead of a spirit of despair...*" ISAIAH 61:2-3 (NIV).

Rejection and abandonment

Almost without exception, dysfunctional adults were subjected to rejection and abandonment throughout childhood, often by people important to them, at times when crucial development should have occurred. The resulting pain is deep, and we sometimes develop a style of anticipating or precipitating rejection as a defense mechanism. We try in this way to protect ourselves from further pain. Unfortunately, it also keeps us from loving and growing. Christ's love turns our rejection into acceptance as we surrender to the belief that he will never reject or abandon us. Christ continually accepts us where we are and takes us where we never dreamed we could go. "*And I will ask the Father, and he will give you another counselor to be with you forever—the Spirit of truth. I will not leave you as orphans; I will come to you.*" JOHN 14:16-18 (NIV).

Fear

Fear is usually present in the lives of adult children. We are afraid of rejection, abandonment, abuse and deprivation; we might even develop an array of phobias. We may have a fear of failure based on having been told repeatedly that we will never amount to anything. For many of us, this fear stopped many of us from believing that the future held any promise. Others avoid success because they feel a need to live up to unrealistic expectations. We may resist accepting responsibilities that we believe are beyond our capabilities.

Our concerns can be faced and subdued as we experience Christ's perfect love for us. In Christ, there is no fear of rejection, abandonment, failure, or the future. As the child within us is nurtured by the Holy Spirit's loving and gentle touch, our misgivings can be dispelled and dissipated. As children of God, we do not need to be afraid because he is always with us, guiding and protecting us. Rather than fear God, we can respect and rely on his presence in our lives. Our reverence for God can gradually overshadow our fears from the past and give us hope for the future. *"Praise be to the Lord, the God of Israel, because he has come and redeemed his people...to rescue us from the hand of our enemies, and to enable us to serve him without fear."* LUKE 1:68,74 (NIV).

Loneliness

Being raised in a dysfunctional home sometimes meant we were left alone to face the world. Even if we weren't literally alone, we were often neglected or ignored. The adults around us often acted as if we weren't even there or paid little or no attention to us.

It is encouraging to realize that with Christ in our lives we never have to be alone again. In Christ-centered recovery, we become a part of his body, the church. *"For we were all baptized by one Spirit into one body—whether Jews or Greeks, slave or free—and we were all given the one Spirit to drink."* 1 CORINTHIANS 12:13 (NIV). Jesus told his disciples that he would never leave them or forsake them.

By recognizing and acknowledging the presence of God in our lives, we can let go of our feelings of loneliness. We may find ourselves physically alone at times, but through prayer, reading and meditation, we can banish our feelings of rejection and come to the peaceful realization that we are never truly alone.

Roots and strongholds

In the midst of our defense mechanisms, adaptations and reactions, we may have allowed negative roots and strongholds to control our lives. Our roots may have been founded on rejection, temporal values, immorality, bitterness, fear and pride. Our strongholds may take the form of character defects, negative attitudes, destructive habits, compulsive behavior and relationship problems. Jesus came to provide new roots and build new strongholds for us. Paul said, *"The weapons we fight with are not the weapons of this world. On the contrary, they have divine power to demolish strongholds. We demolish arguments and every pretension that sets itself up against the knowledge of God, and we take captive every thought to make it obedient to Christ."* 2 CORINTHIANS 10:4-5 (NIV).

These are a few of the specific areas in the lives of adult children that require healing. Our goals should reflect a personal desire for continuous healing, not only in our own lives, but for our families. The healing we are experiencing can influence our entire household and others who are close to us. It is possible for us to become well enough that we can break the cycle of dysfunction that has been passed from one generation to another.

Finally, it is possible for us to come to a place in our lives where we can admit with confidence that we are in recovery and being healed. It is important to recognize that recovery is a slow process. It can only be accomplished one day at a time, for the rest of our lives.

As we proceed on our journey toward wholeness, we need to be aware of possible setbacks. We are especially vulnerable during recovery, for neither can we always see what is being healed, nor can we always accurately observe our progress. Some would have us believe that healing is a reality for everyone but us. But we must remember that if we honestly ask God to help us and are doing his will to the best of our ability, we can become whole.

Individual Exercise

● What behaviors of yours have those close to you pointed out that you tend to deny? _____

_____

_____

_____

_____

_____

● When are you most likely to blame others? Who are you most likely to blame? _____

_____

_____

_____

_____

_____

_____

● What situations cause you to feel or act defensive? _____

_____

_____

_____

_____

_____

_____

- Cite examples of your current behavior that indicate you are "becoming an adult." _____

  _____

  _____

  _____

  _____

  _____

  _____

- In what areas do you wish to become more vulnerable to those close to you and to Christ? _____

  _____

  _____

  _____

  _____

  _____

  _____

- How is the *Prayer of St. Francis* helpful to you in your path toward wholeness? _____

  _____

  _____

  _____

  _____

  _____

  _____

Recovery Tool: Daily Inventory and Quiet Time

Taking a daily personal inventory is designed to help us identify both negative and positive attitudes that we may have expressed in our thoughts and behavior throughout the day. It provides a mirror to reflect the thoughts that motivate our actions. The Bible says: *"for as he thinketh in his heart, so is he..."* PROVERBS 23:7 (KJV). The distorted thinking and damaged emotions that are part of a dysfunctional life do not easily leave our mind and heart. Through the use of daily inventory and quiet time, we gain insight into our behavior and accept God's grace as we experience renewal.

Included in this section is a sample of a *Daily Inventory Log* that can be used each day for a week. (Before you fill out this sample, make extra copies for each week.) The left column lists weaknesses that are common to adult children and that impede our recovery and our relationships. The right column lists the corresponding strengths that we need to emphasize or adopt to "grow up and be an adult."

Before taking the inventory, pray for guidance and honesty. To fill out the sample, mark the column for each day, top to bottom, with either a minus (-) if the weakness predominated that day, or a plus (+) if the stength predominated that day.

We can also tailor our own inventory by making a list of unhealthy thoughts, feelings and behaviors that need to be changed or eliminated from our lives.

After completing the daily inventory, pray for insight and guidance again. It is powerful to ask specifically for the Holy Spirit to change or eliminate our weaknesses and to give thanks for our strengths and the changes we have made. The following steps are helpful in leading us into a prayerful state:

Relax and detach.

Prayer begins when we detach our attention from external distractions and focus on God. It helps to sit in a comfortable position and relax all parts of our body as we prepare to "turn off" outside noises and "tune in" to the voice of the Holy Spirit within our hearts.

Focus attention on the inward chamber room of your heart.

Imagine walking down a stairway leading to the heart's inner chamber where Christ resides. We can ask the Holy Spirit to accompany us so that we can talk face-to-face with him. *"Now faith is the substance of things hoped, the evidence of things not seen."* HEBREWS 11:1 (KJV). *"...he that cometh to God must believe that he is, and that he is a rewarder of them that diligently seek him."* HEBREWS 11:6 (KJV).

Converse with Jesus.

Christ is not only our Savior but also our counselor and guide. He is always ready to forgive us when we ask. *"If any of you lack wisdom, let him ask of God, that giveth to all men liberally, and upbraideth not; and it shall be given him."* JAMES 1:5 (KJV). *"If my people which are called by my name, shall humble themselves, and pray, and seek my face, and turn from their wicked ways; then will I hear from heaven, and will forgive their sin, and will heal their land."* 2 CHRONICLES 7:14 (KJV).

Write Christ's response in your journal.

Be specific in noting insights from the Holy Spirit in your journal. After completing a daily inventory, it is often rewarding to spend additional time in meditation. Ultimately, the inventory becomes second nature and can be done quickly. As we mature in the healing process, we may wish to spend more time in quiet communion with God. This is valuable as we learn to see where and how Christ is contributing to our well-being.

Daily Inventory Log

Weaknesses								Strengths
Watch for (—)	Sun	Mon	Tue	Wed	Thu	Fri	Sat	Strive for (+)
Denied								Admitted
Resented								Forgave
Worried								Trusted
Repressed Anger								Expressed Anger
Was Dishonest								Was Honest
Was Caretaking								Nurtured Self
Controlled Others								Empowered Others
Feared Abandonment								Felt Comfortable Alone
Feared Rejection								Took Risks
Feared Authority								Was Assertive
Suppressed Feelings								Expressed Feelings
Stayed Isolated								Felt Comfortable Socially
Had Low Self-Esteem								Felt Confidence
Was Over-Responsible								Delegated Responsibility
Repressed Sexuality								Communicated Sexual Needs
Felt Self-Pity								Accepted Self
Felt Self-Righteous								Felt Humble
Was Impatient								Was Patient
Blamed Others								Accepted Responsibility
Procrastinated								Did Things on Time
Felt Excessive Guilt								Accepted Forgiveness
Excessively Indulged								Was Moderate or Abstinent
Was Distracted								Concentrated
Forgot God								Communed with God
Always Gave								Learned to Receive
Always Took								Learned to Give

Group Exercise

Refer to page 186 for the *Week Eight* meeting format.

● Before doing the exercises, have someone in the group read the following prayer:

Prayer of St. Francis

Lord, make me an instrument of Thy peace.
Where there is hatred—let me sow love
Where there is injury—pardon
Where there is doubt—faith
Where there is despair—hope
Where there is darkness—light
Where there is sadness—joy
O, Divine Master, grant that I may not so much seek
To be consoled—as to console
To be understood—as to understand
To be loved—as to love
for
It is in giving—that we receive
It is in pardoning—that we are pardoned
It is in dying—that we are born to eternal life.
Amen.

● How do you see yourself as an instrument of God's peace? _____

_____

_____

_____

_____

_____

_____

- In what area of your life do you see hope, light and joy? _____

_____

_____

_____

_____

_____

_____

- What resentment do you wish to turn over to Christ and ask for healing and forgiveness from? _____

_____

_____

_____

_____

_____

_____

- Review your actions of last week as recorded on your *Daily Inventory Log.* In what areas did you perform well? In what areas did you perform poorly? _____

_____

_____

_____

_____

_____

_____

● List ways in which you sensed God's presence as you successfully faced temptation. _____

_____

_____

_____

_____

_____

_____

● What losses in your life do you need to grieve? What assistance can you request from the group in helping you grieve? _____

_____

_____

_____

_____

_____

_____

_____

_____

● What is your prayer request for yourself or others? _____

_____

_____

_____

_____

Complete the following *Family Group Prayer Requests.*

_____ is praying for me.

I am praying for _____ and his/her prayer request is

_____

_____

_____

Chapter Nine

Bringing Our Healing Home

. . . .

*B*y now, most of us are aware that there is a way out of our devastation if we surrender our lives to Christ. As adult children, we don't have to stay stuck in our present struggles or remain paralyzed and handicapped in our relationships or functions. We are now able to recognize that it is God's will for us to be whole. We can feel certain that his desire for us is to be healed by the Holy Spirit. We can "...*take heart, for I have overcome the world.*" JOHN 16:33 (NIV). We are "...*more than conquerors through him who loved us.*" ROMANS 8:37 (NIV).

God wants us to be healthy and mature so we can begin to reach out and bring comfort to our loved ones as we continue to grow. Once we begin to experience recovery, we can offer encouragement, comfort and support to others in our lives who suffer from damaging, pain-filled family systems. "*Praise be to the God and Father of our Lord Jesus Christ, the Father of compassion and the God of all comfort, who comforts us in all our troubles, so that we can comfort those in any trouble with the comfort we ourselves have received from God.*" 2 CORINTHIANS 1:3-4 (NIV).

While moving through our pain and dysfunction into Christ-centered recovery, we start feeling good about ourselves, and our lives become more joyous and productive. It is through our own recovery and our new relationship with Christ that we can begin to have a positive influence on those around us.

It is important to proceed cautiously and gently as we work with other people. We will do well to follow the example of how benevolently Christ works with us. He does not expect us to impose our new lives upon others with a self-righteous attitude; instead, he calls upon us to set a good example as healthy, functional and fulfilled people. "*...I urge you to live a life worthy of the calling you have received. Be completely humble and gentle; be patient, bearing with one another in love.*" EPHESIANS 4:1-2 (NIV).

It is vital to remember that we can only change ourselves and our own behavior. We cannot force change on others, but we can share our lives and our recovery slowly and gently so that by our examples others may see how they might change their lives. "*And be ye kind to one another, tenderhearted, forgiving one other, even as God for Christ's sake hath forgiven you.*" EPHESIANS 4:32 (KJV).

There are three fundamental principles that we need to apply if we are going to experience satisfactory recovery and be able to share our recovery with others. They may be contrary to our previous beliefs and behaviors, but they are critical to our success in becoming healthy role models. These principles are:

— I can change no other person.

— I can only change myself.

— Others can change by seeing and understanding my change.

It is important that we acknowledge and practice these principles in order to set a good example for our family and friends in guiding them toward healthier living.

The following prayer by Reinhold Niebuhr can be a helpful tool for us as we attempt to practice these healthy behaviors.

Prayer for Serenity

God, grant me the serenity
to accept the things I cannot change,
the courage to change the things I can,
and the wisdom to know the difference.
Living one day at a time,

enjoying one moment at a time;
accepting hardship as a pathway to peace;
taking, as Jesus did,
this sinful world as it is,
not as I would have it;
trusting that you will make all things right
if I surrender to your will;
so that I may be reasonably happy in this life
and supremely happy with you forever in the next.
Amen.

It is through consistent serenity, courage and wisdom that we maintain our own recovery. We can let go of others and release them to God's care. We are finally able to trust in his timing and believe that he will care for us and our loved ones. As we surrender our self-will, and focus on changing ourselves instead of others, we model for others the healthy, functional adult life that is now becoming ours in Christ.

We must remember that we cannot change everything all at once. We need to proceed slowly, taking one day at a time and one problem at a time. It helps to become a regular participant in a Christ-centered support group with people who readily identify with the struggles involved in moving from dysfunctional to functional family living. We need to be as open and honest as possible with God, ourselves and those around us. When we can live comfortably in our present reality, our past failures, or future fantasies are more easily accepted and understood.

In order to bring our healing home, there are certain guidelines we can use. If we are willing to focus on these principles, we can expect to see some qualitative shifts within our family system.

Some of these guidelines are:

— Provide healthy, godly role models in our homes.

— Establish clear rules and boundaries for our family's security and protection. Apply these rules equally to every family member, including ourselves. Establish appropriate consequences for violating rules that are consistent and fair.

— Develop an atmosphere of trust, openness, honesty and communication among family members.

— Provide a time and place for family prayer, devotion, worship and celebration.

— Respect the personal space and privacy of everyone in our home.

— Live by a system of priorities that is clearly observed.

— Encourage rest, relaxation, play and creativity.

— Provide an atmosphere of hospitality, warmth and caring for anyone who comes into our home.

— Develop wholesome, meaningful family traditions.

— Refrain from trying to buy love or control and manipulate others with things.

— Provide alternatives for negative influences that come into our home.

— Do away with performance orientation. Let others know they are loved unconditionally.

— Provide opportunities for learning about and forming healthy values, morals and ethics.

— Model healthy nurturing during every stage of our family's development.

— Live by a mutually-agreed-upon covenant with mutual and loving accountability. Make real and vital commitments to family and friends.

Recovery requires the elimination of unhealthy family patterns and the establishment of healthy practices. For a family to be fully functional, there are numerous conditions that must be present. Some of these are:

— Unconditional love and acceptance of one another. (This does not mean condoning unacceptable behavior.)

— Acceptance of problems as being a normal part of life.

— Open communication.

— Clear goals and objectives.

— Consistent and firm guidance and nurture.

— Encouragement and positive affirmation.

— Celebration of one another's joys, accomplishments and growth.

— Comfort for one another's failures, mistakes and losses.

All family members benefit when positive family experiences outnumber negative ones. Giving and receiving hugs is an easy way to communicate warmth, love and good feelings. Families can function well by using words positively for edification, guidance, discipline, sharing and intimacy. Family life stabilizes when we provide structure for our interactions and appropriate expectations for ourselves and others. People thrive in an atmosphere of flexibility, growth and healthy change.

After becoming involved in the recovery process, many of us develop unrealistic expectations of ourselves. When we find they are not being met, we become discouraged and can easily relapse and interrupt the progress we have made. Also, when we are working with others, it is important to stay focused on our own recovery goals.

Following are suggestions for avoiding some of the pitfalls others have experienced in recovery:

Don't place unreal expectations upon ourselves, other family members, or those we are helping in the recovery process.

It is important that we allow ourselves and others to learn from our mistakes. It is not wise to force unreal or premature recovery upon those who are not ready for it. If we are working with family units, we need to let them grow into their maturity naturally, according to God's time table rather than ours.

Trust that maturity and healing are God's will for every family system.

We need not accept the status quo if it is unhealthy or destructive. We can strive for the maturity and healing that are clearly part of the New Testament promise.

Realize that healing is a process.

In most cases, healing takes time, especially when we are working to create new, healthy family systems. The Holy Spirit works in us to heal our inner wounds when we are ready. It helps to trust that God knows what needs healing and when. For our part, we must make a true commitment to change, understanding that pain and effort will be required of us."...*work out your salvation* (healing) *with fear and trembling* (trauma)..." PHILIPPIANS 2:12 (NIV) (parentheses mine).

Acknowledge that maturity is a process.

In recovery, we sometimes tend to be like the child who is seven, going on 17. We want to face the reality of our immaturity one day, and then be perfect in our Christian maturity the next day. If not, we are discouraged with ourselves and everyone around us. Maturity entails a process that is ordained by God. An oak tree does not grow from a sapling to a full-grown tree in one year, and we cannot expect to grow into a fully mature adult overnight.

Jesus confronts this situation in LUKE 13:6-9 (NIV), "...*A man had a fig tree, planted in his vineyard, and he went to look for fruit on it, but did not find any. So he said to the man who took care of the vineyard, 'For three years now, I've been coming to look for fruit on this fig tree and haven't found any. Cut it down! Why should it use up the soil?' 'Sir,' the man replied, 'leave it alone for one more year and I'll dig around it and fertilize it. If it bears fruit next year, fine! If not, then cut it down.'*"

It is important to allow ourselves and others time to mature. We must be nurtured and cared for like the fig tree. God knows what is best for us, and we can safely trust his timetable. If we do, we can be assured that the fruit we bear will be the fruit of the Spirit; "...*love, joy, peace, patience, kindness, goodness, faithfulness, gentleness and self-control...*" GALATIANS 5:22 (NIV).

Don't sidestep the real issues of healing and maturity with defense mechanisms.

When we have been repeatedly hurt, disappointed, or discouraged, our natural tendency is to defend ourselves from further pain. We deny reality by refusing to admit our problems or project the blame for them onto others. In recovery, we can come to believe that Christ is our defender and that we don't need to deny or blame as a protective shield.

Don't mask dysfunction with adaptation.

We learn early in a painful family system how to pretend that everything is normal and right. We adapt ourselves to the situation at hand, believing it is our duty to change, rather than face the reality of our circumstances. The problem is that we develop a warped sense of what is reasonable and accept pain and confusion as normal. We may clown or laugh our way through stressful experiences and sincerely believe that we have emerged untouched. We pretend that what happens in our home is really okay. In so doing, we are adapting instead of changing.

Don't allow functional-dysfunctionalism.

We may come to the conclusion that dysfunction is our lot in life and we might as well get used to it and make the best of it. We learn to cope with our environment by developing skills such as people-pleasing. This is a tragic mistake and does not support healing and maturity. This type of behavior is not a permanent solution to any problem and only provides a temporary escape. We may present a facade of being functional but still be very dysfunctional under the mask of our coping skills. Our insides can be wrenching, while outside we appear happy and cheerful.

Deal with our inclination to be reactionary and judgmental.

Many of us react inappropriately to people, places and things in our past and our present, instead of learning how to respond in a healthy manner. This can lead to bitterness and judgment instead of forgiveness and healing. Jesus said, "*Do not judge, or you too will be judged. For in the same way you judge others, you will be judged, and with the measure you use, it will be measured to you. Why do you look at the speck of sawdust in your brother's eye and pay no attention to the plank in your own eye? How can you say to our brother, 'Let me take the speck out of your eye' when all the time there is a plank in your own eye? You hypocrite, first take the plank out of your own eye, and then you will see clearly to remove the speck from your brother's eye.*" MATTHEW 7:1-5 (NIV).

It is important that we act according to our own motives and remain consistently accountable for them. We can safely leave judgment of others to God.

Maintain clear recovery goals.

The Bible exhorts us to move onward: "*Let us hold unswervingly to the hope we profess, for he who promised is faithful. And let us consider how we may spur one another on toward love and good deeds. Let us not give up meeting together, as some are in the habit of doing, but let us encourage one another—and all the more as you see the Day approaching.*" HEBREWS 10:23-25 (NIV). The day of our wholeness is approaching, and we need to have goals that motivate and encourage us in the direction of maturity and fullness of life in Christ.

Clearly defined recovery goals serve to move us from dysfunction to function, from pain to healing, from immaturity to maturity, from childishness to childlikeness and from despair to glory. We need to give and receive the consistent encouragement and confrontation of other members of the body of Christ to keep us on the path to recovery. In his letter in 1 CORINTHIANS 12:26 (NIV), Paul says, *"If one part suffers, every part suffers with it. If one part is honored, every part rejoices with it."* Our task toward one another is to suffer with those who are suffering and rejoice with those who are rejoicing.

Individual Exercise

- In what areas do those close to you need comforting and healing? __

  _____

  _____

  _____

  _____

  _____

  _____

- Describe two situations that indicate you are "bringing your healing home." _____

  _____

  _____

  _____

  _____

  _____

  _____

- Who in your life do you want to stop judging and relinquish to the care of God? Describe the judgment you need to let go of. _____

  _____

  _____

  _____

  _____

  _____

  _____

● What things in your life that you cannot change do you want to learn to accept? _____

_____

_____

_____

_____

_____

_____

● What are the two most valuable contributions you have recently made to your family? _____

_____

_____

_____

_____

_____

_____

● What is your reaction to the fact that you cannot affect change in others—that you can only change yourself? _____

_____

_____

_____

_____

_____

_____

Recovery Tool: Worship

Worshiping God must have a high priority in our new lives in recovery. "...*Worship the Lord your God and serve him only.*" LUKE 4:8 (NIV). "*Therefore, I urge you, brothers, in view of God's mercy, to offer your bodies as living sacrifices, holy and pleasing to God—this is your spiritual act of worship.*" ROMANS 12:1 (NIV).

Step Three of the Twelve Steps of Alcoholics Anonymous expresses a significant concept that serves as a foundation for worshiping God: "Made a decision to turn our will and our lives over to the care of God *as we understood Him.*" Before we began recovery, many of us may have pursued false gods or used other things in place of a spiritual God. In some cases, the thing we cherished may have been alcohol, drugs, food, or another person. We may have spent a lot of time and energy meeting the demands of these other gods—putting our faith and trust in them. When our lives begin to revolve around these false idols, they can become the primary basis for our values, goals and decisions.

When we "turn our lives over to the care of God," we begin to embrace his standards and values as set forth in the Bible. Life becomes different. Christ becomes the central influence and focus of our lives. "*Delight yourself in the Lord and he will give you the desires of your heart.*" PSALMS 37:4 (NIV). If God is to be the most important influence in our lives, we must be true to him and "*have no other gods before me,*" EXODUS 20:3 (NIV) as we were taught in the Ten Commandments. Worship is one way through which we remove any false gods that we may have previously served.

If we look carefully at our past, we can see how destructive our false gods have been. Through their influence, we may feel guilt or shame about the past, disillusionment with the present and anxiety about the future. God generously forgives the past, gives fulfillment and purpose to the present and extends hope for the future. As we worship God, we become the beneficiaries of these realities.

God calls us to honor him because he loves us and desires that we be whole and healthy. Through worship we encounter the Lord in new and fresh ways. God made us to be in community with all of his creation. Worshiping together strengthens and renews us. When we revere and respect the Lord, the Holy Spirit is released within us uniting the body of Christ in ministry for the common good.

As recovering adult children, worship is vital to our lives. Staying on the road to recovery requires that we maintain a healthy relationship with God, ourselves and others. Veneration humbles us before the Lord, curbing our tendency to be self-centered and prideful. As we turn to Christ, we remove the attention from ourselves and become more in touch with God. During worship, we are open to receiving significant insights. God helps us see our strengths and our successes as well as our weaknesses and shortcomings. Worship enables us to stop blaming other people and accept responsibility for our own attitudes and actions. It helps us see the beauty in all of God's creation as well as the good in ourselves and in others. We praise and thank God for forgiveness, healing and our new lives.

For those who are suffering, there is encouragement. God who comforts us is able to empower us to minister comfort and healing to others. Confusion is dispelled and faith is reinforced as we worship together. There is peace and rejoicing as the surrounding community observes and is drawn into the Kingdom of God. Our worship is not only edifying to those present; it is also a very important means of bringing others into the body of Christ.

Finally, when our lives include worship and praise offered to God, we can concentrate on what is most important to us. We may at times feel overwhelmed by seeing all our problems at once. If we commit to focusing on one issue at a time, we can put our heart, mind and soul into healing that specific area. We can learn to set realistic priorities and deal with each issue in its turn.

Group Exercise

Refer to page 186 for the *Week Nine* meeting format.

- What traditions or rituals are important in your home now? _____

  _____

  _____

  _____

  _____

  _____

- What is your main recovery goal? Describe your progress in attaining this goal. _____

  _____

  _____

  _____

  _____

  _____

- Which fruit of the Spirit (love, joy, peace, patience, kindness, goodness, faithfulness, gentleness and self-control) do you most strongly want to improve upon or introduce into your life? Explain. _____

  _____

  _____

  _____

  _____

  _____

- *"If one falls down, his friends can help him up. But pity the man who falls and has no one to help him up!"* ECCLESIASTES 4:10 (NIV). How does this relate to the work you have done to date with your Christ-centered support group? _____

  _____

  _____

  _____

  _____

  _____

- Share a meaningful experience in using the journal as part of your recovery process. _____

  _____

  _____

  _____

  _____

  _____

- What is your prayer request for yourself or others? _____

  _____

  _____

  _____

  _____

Complete the following *Family Group Prayer Requests.*

_____ is praying for me.

I am praying for _____ and his/her prayer request is

_____

_____

_____

Chapter Ten

Twelve-Step Recovery

. . . .

A twelve-step program is a tool which provides structure for the recovery process, much like a form that is used to pour a concrete foundation. Following the tradition of the early church and the Wesley Revival, the Oxford Group systematized a series of "steps" as a process for cleansing and renewing one's inner life. Some of the concepts of these steps were later adapted by Alcoholics Anonymous, with some of the Christian references deleted. Since the founding of Alcoholics Anonymous in 1935, the Twelve Steps have become a way for many millions of people to change the course of their lives. Participation in a twelve-step program as part of Christ-centered recovery can greatly enhance our spiritual progress.

The Twelve Steps are not sponsored by any particular religious group or entity. Though people using this program find it harmonious with their own personal theology and spiritual beliefs, it has no official religious affiliation. It is, however, a program that helps us rediscover and deepen the spiritual part of ourselves and recognize its importance in our lives. It is a valuable tool for Christians who are working to renew and strengthen their relationship with their Higher Power, Jesus Christ.

With God's presence, a twelve-step program becomes an empowering tool to relieve our suffering and fill our emptiness. Used in Christ-centered recovery, it helps us to experience more energy, love and joy in ways we have not known before. It is a process that we follow at our own pace, in our own way, with God's help and the support of others who are in recovery.

The purpose of using the Twelve Steps as a tool in Christ-centered recovery is to bring to light biblical insights which can be integrated into our spiritual pilgrimage and show us a new way of relating to God in our daily lives. As we work through the issues interfering with our lives, we see where the Steps are a progressive means of renewing our relationship with God.

Trust in God's guidance is necessary when implementing the Steps as a part of our recovery. Twelve-step material which has been adapted for Christ-centered recovery groups can be found in *The Twelve Steps for Christians*. The companion workbook, *The Twelve Steps—A Spiritual Journey*, is written within a twelve-step framework, upon which our own life experiences can be reviewed with love and courage.

The Twelve Steps—A Spiritual Journey is a comprehensive working guide that enables the user to gain an understanding of the spiritual power of the Twelve Steps when worked within a Christian perspective. If you have gained value and insights from *When I Grow Up* . . . **I Want To Be An Adult**, additional benefits can be attained by continuing the process using *The Twelve Steps—A Spiritual Journey*.

Following is an adaptation of the Twelve Steps as presented in *The Twelve Steps for Christians*. They are intended for use in Christ-centered recovery groups, and are accompanied by scriptural reference with a brief paragraph about the theme of the Step.

Step One

We admitted we were powerless over the effects of our separation from God—that our lives had become unmanageable.

"I know nothing good lives in me, that is in my sinful nature. For I have the desire to do what is good, but I cannot carry it out."

(ROMANS 7:18)

Step One forms the foundation for working the other Steps. Admitting our powerlessness and accepting the unmanageability of our lives is not an easy thing to do. Although our behavior has caused us stress and pain, it is difficult to let go and trust that our lives can work out well. The idea that there are areas over which we are powerless is a new concept for us. It is much easier for us to feel that we have power and are in control.

Paul the Apostle, in his letter to the Church of Rome, describes his powerlessness and the unmanageability of his life. He writes of his continued sinful behavior as a manifestation of his separation from God. *"We know that the law is spiritual; but I am unspiritual, sold as a slave to sin."* ROMANS 7:14 (NIV). His acknowledgement of his powerlessness does not interfere with his commitment to do God's will. We can conclude from his writing that his self-will was a detriment to his functioning effectively.

Step Two

Came to believe that a power greater than ourselves could restore us to sanity.

"For it is God who works in you to will and to act according to his good purpose."

(PHILIPPIANS 2:13)

Step Two is referred to as the Hope Step. It gives us new hope to see that help is available to us if we simply reach out and accept what our Higher Power, Jesus Christ, has to offer. It is here that we form the foundation for growth of our spiritual life, which helps us become the person we want to be. What is required of us is a willingness to believe that a power greater than ourselves is waiting to be our personal Savior. What follows as we proceed through the Steps is a process that brings Jesus Christ into our lives and enables us to grow in love, health and grace.

One of the great paradoxes of Christianity is that we are not completely free until we have become totally submissive. In JOHN 8:32 (NIV), Jesus made a promise when he said, *"You will know the truth and the truth will set you free."* In this step, we begin to recognize that God does, in fact, have the power and intention to alter the course of our lives. In the Scriptures, we are assured of God's presence within us. We are shown beyond all doubt that through him all things are possible. If you have accepted the truth regarding your condition and are ready to surrender to Jesus Christ, you are well on your way to ultimate submission and true spiritual freedom.

Step Three

Made a decision to turn our will and our lives over to the care of God as we understood Him.

"Therefore, I urge you, brothers, in view of God's mercy, to offer your bodies as living sacrifices, holy and pleasing to God— which is your spiritual worship."

(ROMANS 12:1).

Step Three is an affirmative step. It is time to make a decision. In the first two Steps, we became aware of our condition and accepted the idea of a power greater than ourselves. Although we began to know and trust God, we may find it difficult to think of allowing him to be totally in charge of our lives. However, if the alternative is facing the loss of something critical to our existence, such as family, job, health, or sanity, God's guidance might be easier to accept. Right now, our lives may have many beautiful and rewarding relationships which are being ruined by our addictive and compulsive behavior. We must not allow these discoveries to stop us from moving ahead.

In Step Three we make an important decision by acknowledging that we need God's presence in our lives and giving ourselves to him. We make the decision to surrender our lives to God, make him our new manager and accept life on his terms. Christ exemplifies "turning it over:" *"Going a little farther, he fell with his face to the ground and prayed, 'My Father, if it is possible, may this cup be taken from me. Yet not as I will, but as you will.'"* MATTHEW 23:30 (NIV). During his life on earth, Jesus' love for us led him into constant confrontations with the forces of evil. He was strong and steadfast because he placed his trust in God. We, too, can be strong in the face of trial and temptation because we know that God never abandons us.

Step Four

Made a searching and fearless moral inventory of ourselves.

*"Let us examine our ways and test them, and
let us return to the Lord."*

(LAMENTATIONS 3:40)

Step Four begins the growth part of our journey. Here, we examine our behavior and expand our understanding of ourselves. The adventure of self-discovery begins with Step Four. Being totally honest in preparing our inventory allows us to remove the obstacles that have prevented us from knowing ourselves and truthfully acknowledging our deepest feelings about life.

To examine our ways and test them is similar to cleaning a closet. We take stock of what we have, examine what we want to save and discard what is no longer useful or appropriate. It doesn't have to be done all at once, but it does have to be done eventually. Turning to our Lord for guidance can give us the confidence to proceed with each item. We must remember that the past is only history. It is not the purpose of our inventory to dwell on the past. As described in 2 CORINTHIANS 13:5-6 (NIV), *"Examine yourselves to see whether you are in the faith; test yourselves. Do you not realize that Christ Jesus is in you—unless, of course, you fail the test?"* This step is a tool to help us understand our current behavior patterns and recognize our need for God's guidance in our lives.

Step Five

Admitted to God, to ourselves, and to another human being the exact nature of our wrongs.

"Therefore confess your sins to each other and pray for each other so that you may be healed."

(JAMES 5:16)

Step Five requires that we engage in honest confrontations with ourselves and others by admitting our faults to God, to ourselves and to another person. By doing so, we begin the important phase of setting aside our pride so that we can see ourselves in true perspective. We also realize how our growing relationship with God gives us the courage to examine ourselves, accept who we are and reveal our true selves. Step Five helps us acknowledge and discard our old survival skills and move toward a new and healthier life. Being thorough and honest in completing our inventory places us in a position to face the facts and move forward.

Admitting our wrongs to another human being is the most powerful part of Step Five. It is a true exercise in humility and will help us break down our defenses. Being rigorously honest with another person may be frightening enough to cause us to procrastinate in completing this portion of Step Five. It is tempting to believe that telling God is all that is necessary, because he ultimately forgives all sins. While this is true, it comes after our admission to ourselves and sharing with someone else, for this is where our sense of self-worth begins.

Step Six

Were entirely ready to have God remove all these defects of character.

"Humble yourselves before the Lord, and he will lift you up."

(JAMES 4:10)

The task of removing our ineffective behavior is more than we can handle alone. Step Six does not indicate that we are the ones to do the removing; all we have to do is be "entirely ready" for it to happen. It is a state of being we reach by faithfully working the Steps, whether or not we feel like we are making progress. When we are entirely ready, we become more willing to let God assist us in removing our shortcomings.

In preparing to have our character defects removed, we see that they are familiar tools to us, and losing them threatens our capacity to control ourselves and others. To be lifted up by our Lord means we can trust that God won't remove anything we need. This can create a sense of comfort in us. The smallest beginning is acceptable to God. Jesus tells us that faith is a powerful force. He replied, *"Because you have so little faith. I tell you the truth, if you have faith as small as a mustard seed, you can say to this mountain, 'Move from here to there' and it will move. Nothing will be impossible for you."* MATTHEW 17:20 (NIV). When we have planted our seed of willingness, we need to protect the tiny sprouts of positive results. We do not want the weeds of self-will to overrun our new garden.

Step Seven

Humbly asked Him to remove our shortcomings.

*"If we confess our sins, he is faithful and just
and will forgive us our sins..."*

(1 JOHN 1:9)

Humility is a recurring theme in a twelve-step program, and the central idea of Step Seven. By practicing humility we receive the strength necessary to work the Steps and achieve satisfactory results. We recognize now, more than ever before, that a major portion of our lives has been devoted to fulfilling our self-centered desires. We must set aside these prideful, selfish behavior patterns, come to terms with our inadequacies and realize that humility frees our spirit. Step Seven requires surrendering our will to God so that we may receive the serenity necessary to achieve the happiness we seek.

As we begin to see our defects being removed, and our lives becoming less complicated, we must proceed with caution and guard against the temptation to be prideful. Sudden changes in our behavior can and do happen, but we cannot anticipate them or direct them. God initiates change when we are ready, and we cannot claim that we alone removed our character defects. When we learn to ask humbly for God's help in our lives, change becomes God's responsibility, and we cannot accept the credit. This notion is conveyed in PSALM 51:1-2 (NIV). *"Have mercy on me, O God, according to your unfailing love; according to your great compassion blot out my transgressions. Wash away all my iniquity and cleanse me from my sin."*

Step Eight

Made a list of all persons we had harmed and became willing to make amends to them all.

"Do to others as you would have them do to you."

(LUKE 6:31)

Step Eight begins the process of healing damaged relationships through our willingness to make amends for past misdeeds. We can let go of our resentments and start to overcome the guilt, shame and low self-esteem we have acquired through our harmful actions. We can leave the gray, angry world of loneliness behind and move toward a bright future by exercising our newly developed relating skills. Through the gift of the Twelve Steps, we have the necessary tools to overcome these damaging conditions and mend our broken friendships.

It is important that Christians endeavor to have and maintain deep, loving relationships. Through Christ's example, we see how he devoted his ministry to loving people and encouraged them to love one another. Jesus taught that being reconciled to God requires reconciliation with other human beings. In Step Eight, we prepare ourselves to carry out God's master plan for our lives by becoming willing to make amends. *"You, therefore, have no excuse, you who pass judgment on someone else, for at whatever point you judge the other, you are condemning yourself, because you who pass judgement do the same things."* ROMANS 2:1 (NIV). Once we have prepared our list of those whom we have harmed, we are able to extend our love and acceptance not only to the injured persons, but to all other members of God's family.

Step Nine

Made direct amends to such people wherever possible, except when to do so would injure them or others.

*"Therefore, if you are offering your gift at the altar
and there remember that your brother has something against you, leave your gift there in front
of the altar. First go and be reconciled to your
brother; then come and offer your gift."*

(MATTHEW 5:23-24)

Step Nine completes the forgiveness process that began in Step Four and fulfills our requirement to reconcile with others. In this Step, we clear our "garden" of dead leaves and "rake up and discard" the old habits. We are ready to face our faults, to admit the extent of our wrongs, and to ask for and extend forgiveness. Accepting responsibility for the harm done can be an awkward experience, as it forces us to admit the effect we have had on others.

Before we can truly be reconciled with God, we must be reconciled to our brothers and sisters. Judging others separates us from them and prevents us from extending the love to one another that God commands of us. *"Above all, love each other deeply, because love covers over a multitude of sins. Offer hospitality to one another without grumbling. Each one should use whatever gift he has received to serve others, faithfully administering God's grace in its various forms."* 1 PETER 4:8-10 (NIV). This Step is a reminder that we receive God's grace without having to earn it. We must offer goodness to others in the same manner, expecting nothing in return.

Step Ten

Continued to take personal inventory and, when we were wrong, promptly admitted it.

"So, if you think you are standing firm, be careful that you don't fall."

(1 CORINTHIANS 10:12)

In Step Ten, we begin the maintenance segment of the Steps. We will learn how to sustain what we have accomplished, become more confident, and proceed with joy along our spiritual journey. The first nine steps put our house in order and enable us to change some of our destructive behavior patterns. By continuing to work the Steps, we increase our capacity to develop new and healthier ways of taking care of ourselves and relating to others.

The Steps and Scripture repeatedly remind us that God is in charge, and that our new state of mind is grounded in what God wants for us, rather than in what we want for ourselves. *"You were taught, with regard to your former way of life, to put off your old self, which is being corrupted by its deceitful desires; to be made new in the attitude of your minds; and to put on the new self, created to be like God in true righteousness and holiness."* EPHESIANS 4:22-24 (NIV). Keeping this in our mind can prevent us from "falling." As we complete Step Ten, we must not be over-confident in our recovery. Slipping into past behaviors can endanger our commitment to do God's will. The work we do in the twelve-step program basically provides a structure wherein we can look at ourselves with honesty and lovingly accept who we are.

Step Eleven

Sought through prayer and meditation to improve
our conscious contact with God as we understood
Him, praying only for knowledge of his will for
us and the power to carry that out.

"Let the work of Christ dwell in you richly."
(COLOSSIANS 3:16)

To protect what we have learned, we must continually seek to know God's will for us. A daily regimen of prayer and meditation makes it clear that relief from pain of the past is just a day-to-day reprieve—we must relentlessly pursue recovery on a daily basis. Those of us who have experienced the hell and chaos caused by our willful acts realize that we may have worshipped false gods such as drugs, sex, or money and were often participants in addictive relationships. For us, surrendering to the Twelve Steps was not what directed us toward heaven, but was, in fact, what led us out of the hell that our lives had become.

Christ can dwell in us richly as we fulfill our commitment to work the Twelve Steps. By being attentive to our own needs and trusting in God completely, our spiritual and emotional development are enhanced. God can lead us toward healing and wholeness as described in PSALM 25:4-5 (NIV): *"Show me your ways, O LORD, teach me your paths; guide me in your truth and teach me, for you are God my Savior, and my hope is in you all day long."* Giving thanks for all our opportunities to serve the Lord heightens our sensitivity to the infinite ways in which he is leading us.

Step Twelve

Having had a spiritual awakening as the result of these steps, we tried to carry this message to others, and to practice these principles in all our affairs.

"Brothers, if someone is caught in a sin, you who are spiritual should restore him gently. But watch yourself, or you also may be tempted."

(GALATIANS 6:1)

Step Twelve reminds us that we have not completed our journey to wholeness. To continue our process of growth, we must be aware that we have just begun to learn the principles that enhance our walk with the Lord. Each of the Twelve Steps is a vital part of fulfilling God's plan for us. Conscientious attention to working the Steps develops in us a level of love, acceptance, honesty and peace of mind unequalled at any other time in our lives. The hardest part of any journey is the beginning, and we have taken that step through our commitment to recovery.

Now we have the opportunity to promote our own growth by helping others. Our willingness to share our commitment to recovery and our growing awareness of God's presence in our lives keep us ever-vigilant for ways to share our new confidence. This program calls us to take responsibility for the daily application of our values to our lives. The Apostle Paul clearly instructed us in this action by saying: *"But in your hearts set apart Christ as Lord. Always be prepared to give an answer to everyone who asks you to give the reason for the hope that you have. But do this with gentleness and respect..."* 1 PETER 3:15 (NIV).

The fact that God's plan for us is revealed in the Holy Scriptures is easily accepted by those of us who are Christians. Both mature Christians and those who are just being awakened to a personal relationship with God can find tremendous value in the Twelve Steps. By applying them to the events of our lives on a daily basis, they become an effective means for enriching our relationship with God and allowing his plan for us to unfold. The Steps are powerful when used with Christian practices of prayer and Bible study. We discover the unique ways in which God's word supports and expands our understanding of the Steps.

Completing this book is an important step toward preparing to effectively work the Twelve Steps. Being aware of the impactful events in our developmental history can help us to understand some of our current behaviors and recognize that changes are necessary. The Twelve Steps represent a spiritual discipline that helps us to accept life's challenges, one day at a time.

The recovery process is a journey that takes time, commitment and diligence. Willingness to continue our recovery by entering into the next phase and using the Twelve Steps in our lives can significantly benefit us. We will discover new or improved skills in effectively relating to ourselves and others. We will be able to re-examine our relationship with God and discover ways in which he can empower our daily lives. We will learn to look fearlessly at the "shadow" side of our personalities, and accept our unwanted tendencies such as inappropriately expressed anger, sexual behavior, hostility, or aggression. It is important to remember that this process includes inviting Jesus to help us redefine the limits we set for ourselves as we discover that all things are possible for those who love the Lord. The twelve-step process of recovery is a spiritual journey, and is valuable when used within the context of Christ-centered support groups. If you wish to proceed further in your recovery process, it is recommended that you join a twelve-step group in your church or community. A list of *Self-Help Resources* can be found in *Appendix Four* on page 193.

Concluding Individual Exercise

● How do you see the Twelve Steps as a valuable tool in furthering your journey toward healing and wholeness? _____

_____

_____

_____

_____

● What commitment are you willing to make to yourself to continue your recovery and proceed with using the Steps as part of your healing process? _____

_____

_____

_____

_____

_____

● In what ways do you feel that the Twelve Steps are compatible with Christianity? Cite two examples. _____

_____

_____

_____

_____

_____

Recovery Tool: The Twelve Steps—A Spiritual Discipline

Discipline, as defined by Webster's Dictionary, originates from the root word disciple. As Christians we are disciples, or followers of Jesus Christ. As followers we seek to model ourselves after him so we can develop the self-control, character and orderliness of Jesus. Seeking to do God's will is a repeating theme throughout his teachings. This chapter illustrates how working the Twelve Steps as part of our recovery journey helps us accept God's authority in our lives.

The Twelve Steps are an effective tool in dealing with life's painful and complex issues. They are compatible with Christian beliefs and represent a spiritual discipline for all Christians. *The Twelve Steps for Christians* and *The Twelve Steps—A Spiritual Journey* are books pertaining to adult children who were raised in addictive or other dysfunctional families. They emphasize the important relationship between the Twelve Steps and the practice of Christianity.

The following exercise is an abbreviated summary of the process used in *The Twelve Steps—A Spiritual Journey*.

- Identify a situation or condition in your life that is currently a source of resentment, fear, sadness, or anger. It may involve relationships (family, work, sexual), work environment, health, or self-esteem. Write a concise statement describing the situation and indicating your concern. _____

_____

_____

_____

Submission

Step One: *We admitted we were powerless over the effects of our separation from God—that our lives had become unmanageable.*

- In what ways are you powerless, and how is this situation showing you the unmanageability of your life? _____

_____

_____

_____

Conversion

Step Two: *Came to believe that a power greater than ourselves could restore us to sanity.*
- How can Jesus Christ help to restore you to sanity? _____
_____
_____
_____
_____

Step Three: *Made a decision to turn our will and our lives over to the care of God as we understood Him.*
- How does being willing to turn your life over to the care of God assist you in dealing with this? _____
_____
_____
_____

Confession

Step Four: *Made a searching and fearless moral inventory of ourselves.*
- What character defects have caused the most damage in your life? Explain (e.g., fear of abandonment or authority figures, control, obsessive/compulsive behavior, excessive responsibility, unexpressed feelings)._____
_____
_____
_____
_____

Step Five: *Admitted to God, to ourselves, and to another human being the exact nature of our wrongs.*
- Admit your wrongs, at least to God and to yourself. _____
_____
_____
_____
_____

Repentance

Step Six: *Were entirely ready to have God remove all these defects of character.*

- Are you entirely ready to have God remove the character defects that surfaced in Step Four? If not, explain. _____

_____

_____

_____

_____

Step Seven: *Humbly asked Him to remove our shortcomings.*

- Can you humbly submit to God and ask him to remove your shortcomings? If not, why do you resist? _____

_____

_____

_____

_____

_____

Amends

Step Eight: *Made a list of all persons we had harmed and became willing to make amends to them all.*

- Make a list of the persons you have harmed._____

_____

_____

_____

_____

Step Nine: *Made direct amends to such people wherever possible, except when to do so would injure them or others.*

- What amends are necessary, and how will you make them? _____

_____

_____

_____

_____

Confession

Step Ten: *Continued to take personal inventory and, when we were wrong, promptly admitted it.*

- What did you do today that requires admitting your wrongs? ___

_____

_____

_____

_____

Prayer

Step Eleven: *Sought through prayer and meditation to improve our conscious contact with God as we understood Him, praying only for knowledge of His will for us and the power to carry that out.*

- Take a moment and ask God for knowledge of his will for you. What is your understanding of God's will in this situation? _____

_____

_____

_____

_____

Ministry

Step Twelve: *Having had a spiritual awakening as the result of these steps, we tried to carry this message to others, and to practice these principles in all our affairs.*

- How can your understanding and spiritual awakening assist you in dealing more effectively with your life? _____

_____

_____

_____

_____

Concluding Group Exercise

Prior to discussing the concluding exercise with your family group, share your writing from this week's individual exercise.

- Write a brief summary of the benefits you received from participating in this group. Include your most memorable experiences and describe your feelings as a result of these experiences. _____

  _____

  _____

  _____

  _____

  _____

  _____

- What would you like to share with your family group members during this final meeting? _____

  _____

  _____

  _____

  _____

  _____

Appendix One

Seeking Help

The primary purpose of this book is to illustrate how to transform self-defeating behaviors into effective behaviors through the support of Christ-centered recovery groups. With God's help, wounded people in these groups have been assisting each other to significantly alter destructive life patterns. Receiving support is an important element of recovery and is an essential element in correcting the behaviors which hurt us and others. Encouraging recovering friends is important because it reminds us of our own ongoing struggle. Others can benefit when we share our experience, strength and hope with them.

There are various ways to begin the process of recovery. We can do it with a support group, a sponsor, a pastor who understands dysfunctional family systems, or with a professional therapist trained in this area. Many of us have tried to cope with our destructive behavior alone and found it overpowering. Self-will cannot free us from the trap in which we have found ourselves, and help must be sought from other sources. The first step in seeking assistance is a sincere willingness to be rigorously honest with ourselves.

In some cases professional counseling is desired as part of the recovery process. The following excerpts taken from *Can Christians Love Too Much?—Breaking the Cycle of Codependence* (Zondervan Publishing House, 1989) will be helpful. In this book, Dr. Margaret Rinck outlines her professional experiences in treating addictive, compulsive and obsessive people in therapy. She points out that any treatment program must address particular aspects of the behavior. After spending time exploring your current behaviors, a trained professional may ask some of the following questions:

— What happens that triggers self-defeating behavior?
— What do you keep doing in spite of your knowing it hurts you and other people?
— What sort of behaviors do you engage in that violate your Christian values? How does this violation of values affect your relationships at home and at work?
— How does your destructive behavior affect your self-esteem and finances? What toll has it taken on your health, emotions and spiritual life?
— How do you keep yourself from going off the deep end when you are not feeling good about yourself?
— How does depression and anxiety affect your sleep, diet and physical health? Have you thought about hurting yourself?

— What rationalizations do you use to justify addictive, compulsive, or obsessive behavior? In what way are you denying reality?

— How do you excessively focus on the object of your addiction?

In treatment, the client and therapist work as a team to begin the process of building new thinking and behavior skills. Instead of self-defeating behavior being a source of frustration, awareness of it can help us to discover other opinions which can assist the healing process. Buried emotions, sometimes painful, are identified and experienced so as to further assist the client in effectively coping with situations which used to be a source of frustration. The overall goal of therapy is for clients to review their lives and begin to implement new skills in thinking and behaving.

Asking for help is not easy for many recovering people. It is not uncommon to feel fearful of becoming overly sad, angry, or ashamed. If there is fear of "losing control," remember that God works in many wonderful and mysterious ways. Trust begins to develop as we step forward to confront our self-defeating behaviors. It is often through others that we can discover alternatives for handling life's problems and can experience Christ's presence in our own lives.

Following are Dr. Rinck's answers to some common questions and concerns voiced by others prior to entering professional therapy:

- *"But I am so ashamed. How could I tell a stranger all these stupid things that I have done?"*

    "Believe me, therapists are human too, and have done stupid things themselves. Also, there is little that a therapist has not heard at one time or another. You may feel as if your story is too unique, bizarre, or sinful, but you may be sure that your therapist may have heard it before! And if he hasn't, he'll refer you to someone else who has experience with your problem."

- *"But I can't afford therapy!"*

    "Let me ask you these questions: Is your emotional, spiritual, mental, or physical health worth the cost of two TV sets and a VCR? If your child needed therapy, would you find a way somehow? Why are you worth less than they are? Also, for those who have low income, all public and some private mental health agencies offer some form of a 'sliding scale' where you pay only what you can afford. Many people find that their health insurance covers fifty to ninety percent of their fee for therapy. Most professional therapists are open to doing some 'pro-bono' work (work for which they do not charge). Some churches also give scholarships for people who legitimately cannot afford therapy; other churches have professional therapists on their staff and offer free services to church members and/or people from the community. And the

Salvation Army and other groups like Women Helping Women offer special types of counseling at little or no cost to you."

- *"I don't know what to look for in a therapist."*

"There are certain things you will want to look for in a therapist, Christian or not. Ask them if they:

have worked in out-patient treatment facilities, and what do they know about codependency and addiction recovery work?

are certified and licensed by your state.

have cognitive-oriented style of therapy.

are open to referring you, when it is appropriate, to group therapy, workshops, twelve-step programs, or other resources if necessary.

work with 'inner child and grief/loss issues'" What is their approach? (You want someone who can facilitate the release of long pent-up feelings as well as teach you new skills.)

have a working relationship with a psychiatrist or medical doctor should medications be necessary.

will tell you what methods they use in therapy."

Following are questions Dr. Rinck suggests that you ask yourself after the first session:

- *"How did I relate to the therapist? Do I need another session or two to really decide if I will 'hit it off' with the therapist, or do I need to find someone else? Did the therapist express positive views regarding the possiblilty of working together?"*

"If you had any questions that went unanswered, or were hesitant to bring up, write them down and be sure to bring them up at the next visit. The patient-therapist relationship is a good predictor for how therapy will go. So finding the 'right fit' is important. Be sure not to worry about their feelings. Some people interview three or four therapists before they pick the one with whom to work. Professionals understand this fact and are not offended if you choose to go elsewhere. Many will even give you a list of names to try."

- *"Do I agree with his methods, and do they seem to be working for me?"*

"Is the therapist respectful of your Christian beliefs? Does he understand them sufficiently to be of help to you? Many non-Christian therapists will respect your faith and, though they are not personally acquainted with it, may be able to work well with you. Some Christian therapists, while genuine believers, do not integrate their beliefs into their therapy at all; others integrate it thoroughly. You have a right to ask what they do."

- **"Does this therapist see me as an active participant in the therapy? Or does he come across as if I am to do just what he says with no input as to goals or type of treatment offered?"**

    "We tell clients that the more that they put into therapy, the more they will get out of it, and that we expect their active participation."

- **"What are my goals for therapy? What do I want to accomplish? Does this therapist seem qualified to meet my needs?"**

    "Generally, there are three types of therapists: psychiatrists, psychologists, and various masters-level people. Psychiatrists are medical doctors who can prescribe medicine as well as do therapy. Some are interested in doing therapy; others prefer only to work with medications, referring the actual therapy to others. Psychologists are also doctoral level people who have been licensed by the state to practice psychology. They are not qualified to give medications."

The recovery process involves a number of resources from which benefits can be derived. These options include a Christ-centered support group, a twelve-step program, therapy, spiritual development, family life, or relationships which include friends at church, work and school. The process began when completing this book. The process will continue for the rest of our lives, one day at a time.

Guidelines for Forming and
Leading a Study Group

*B*efore proceeding with this material, it is important to review *How to Benefit Most from This Book* (page xvii) before proceeding.

Starting a study group is not difficult. You can publicize the meeting by making announcements at other support group meetings and by placing a notice in your church bulletin. Tell your friends about the study group and ask them to participate in it. It is also helpful to distribute copies of the meeting notice to interested persons. Refer to the *Suggested Meeting Announcement* on page 168 for ideas on how to announce the meeting.

The program is designed to last ten weeks. The first meeting is an introductory session that allows individuals to experience the format of the program. It is an opportunity to introduce the material to potential participants and allows time to discuss the value of support groups as part of the recovery process. This meeting offers those who want more information about the program a chance to make a decision about attending the study group. Some people may attend only once and decide not to return. At the *Week One* (Chapter One) meeting, make an announcement that the remaining sessions will be closed to newcomers.

Even though you start the study group and may function as the facilitator, it is helpful to have a different leader each week. It is recommended that leadership rotate by "family group" rather than by individuals. This gives each family group an opportunity to provide leadership periodically. The meeting formats included in *Appendix Three* have proven to be effective, but they are intended as suggestions only. Keep the format simple so study group participants can focus on completing the writing exercises and sharing their experiences and feelings.

In some cases, participants will decide to discontinue their involvement in the program. If a family group diminishes to two or three people, other family groups can "adopt them." This encourages the remaining members of a diminishing group to continue participating in the program without feeling abandoned.

Group leadership requires an awareness of the dynamics of group interaction. Remember that some participants may experience stress or discomfort as a result of working the material. When people get in touch with very painful issues, especially for the first time, they may become emotional and begin to cry. It is important to be patient and allow them to release their emotions. Rather than interrupt the session, continue sharing, accepting the participant's sadness as a natural and appropriate part of the healing process. If the situation appears serious, guide them toward seeking additional outside help (e.g., church counselor, minister, or therapist). This is an opportunity for individuals to become aware of their own needs through sharing with others who have similar problems. It is not designed to be a substitute for professional therapy.

An effective leader encourages group members to listen to each other carefully without giving advice or offering direction. For example, someone in your group may criticize, advise, or confront another participant in a hurtful or inappropriate way. If the person being confronted does not know how to accept criticism and respond in a healthy way, he or she may become overly cautious and withdraw. This inhibits the individual's ability to be open and honest.

It is important to limit "crosstalk" which is when two people enter into a dialogue that excludes other group members and becomes advice giving. Remind people that sharing their experience, strength and hope with others in the group is the best form of encouragement.

The function of the facilitator is to convene and moderate the meetings, assuring that each session flows smoothly. This individual should be loving, supportive and attentive to the needs of the group. He or she should maintain a genuine concern for fellow participants and provide a sense of security and cohesiveness within the group.

The role of the facilitator is to provide support, direction and encouragement to the participants. It is important to realize that this is not group therapy where professional advice is given; it is an arena where individuals can share their own experience, strength and hope.

The facilitator serves as a resource for answering questions relative to the material. This individual offers an element of security wherein group members know that they have someone to turn to when problems arise. The facilitator is not assigned to a specific family group, but rotates each week and participates with the group leading the meeting. This gives the facilitator an opportunity to relate to all members and be attentive to everyone's needs.

The following are suggested guidelines for the facilitator to follow:

Support open communication among participants by:

— Truly listening to what is said.
— Encouraging expression of ideas and feelings.
— Exercising patience and empathy.
— Rewarding honesty and openness with affirmation.

Promote a sense of cohesiveness and unity within the group by:

— Assisting members to rely on the Holy Spirit.
— Focusing on harmony as a priority in the group process.
— Encouraging trust and loyalty.

Demonstrate recovery-type sharing by:

— Relating to group members on their level of recovery.
— Promoting sharing on a feeling level.
— Using your own experiences as a means to communicate ideas and feelings.

Make an effort to resolve conflicts by:

— Being confrontive in a loving way.
— Encouraging honest and open communication.
— Providing a non-threatening atmosphere for individuals to share their discomfort.

The following items are required to form this study group:

— Copies of *When I Grow Up . . . I Want To Be An Adult* available for purchase.
— A meeting place.
— An audio cassette player.
— Relaxing music tapes.
— Copies of the *Introductory Meeting* for attendees who do not have a book.
— 3x5 index cards.

Each session is designed to last two hours. A *Suggested Study Group Meeting Format* for each week is included in *Appendix Three*. The basic design for each session follows:

7:00	Opening
7:10	Writing Exercise
7:25	Family Group Sharing
8:10	Family Group Prayer Requests
8:25	Meeting Break
8:35	Large Group Sharing
8:55	Closing
9:00	Adjourn

Suggested Meeting Announcement

Christ-Centered Study Group
Based on
When I Grow Up . . . I Want To Be An Adult

The First Chuch of San Diego is sponsoring a study group for individuals who grew up in emotionally repressive and dysfunctional families. This is a Christ-centered support group.

Beginning Date: June 4, 1991   **Day:** Wednesday   **Time:** 7 to 9 P.M.

Location: 123 "A" Street, San Diego **Contact Person:** Ron **Phone:** (619) 555-1212

When I Grow Up . . . I Want To Be An Adult is written for adult Christians who were raised in dysfunctional homes. An empowering book, it aims to provide all Christians with hope and direction on their Christ-centered recovery journey. The author, Ron Ross, provides individual and group exercises which assist participants in overcoming their problems and, with God's help, transform their self-defeating behavior.

Study Group Overview

Following is an outline of what to expect from participating in this study group using the book *When I Grow Up* . . . I Want To Be An Adult.

— During the *Introductory Meeting* and *Week One* (Chapter One), the meeting remains open to newcomers so that anyone interested in becoming familiar with the meeting format is welcome to do so.

— During *Week Two* (Chapter Two), small family groups are formed. They are an important part of the study group process and encourage the development of trusting, supportive relationships during the weeks that follow.

— One week is devoted to each chapter.

— Read the chapter material and complete the *Individual Exercise* prior to the group meeting.

— The *Group Exercise* at the end of each chapter is the focus of the weekly meeting. Time is spent at the beginning of the meeting to complete the exercise, which then becomes the basis for sharing.

— An important reminder is that you are doing this work for your own personal growth. Set your own pace and accept your progress without having unrealistic expectations of yourself.

— This program is worked most successfully one day at a time.

Suggested Meeting Schedule

Christ-Centered Study Group
When I Grow Up . . . I Want To Be An Adult
Program Schedule

Week	Date	In-Class Exercise	At-Home Work
Intro	6/04	Introductory Meeting	Chapter One
1	6/11	Chapter One Who Am I?	Chapter Two
2	6/18	Chapter Two Pain Insulataors	Chapter Three
3	6/25	Chapter Three Stunted Growth	Chapter Four
4	7/02	Chapter Four Trusting Our Senses	Chapter Five
5	7/09	Chapter Five The Healing Touch	Chapter Six
6	7/16	Chapter Six Becoming Childlike	Chapter Seven
7	7/23	Chapter Seven Becoming Christ-Centered	Chapter Eight
8	7/30	Chapter Eight Becoming an Adult	Chapter Nine
9	8/06	Chapter Nine Bringing Our Healing Home	Chapter Ten
10	8/13	Chapter Ten Twelve-Step Recovery	

Suggested Family Group Roster

Christ-Centered Study Group
When I Grow Up . . . I Want To Be An Adult

Facilitator _____ Phone # _____

Family #1		Family #2	
Name	Phone #	Name	Phone #
_____	_____	_____	_____
_____	_____	_____	_____
_____	_____	_____	_____
_____	_____	_____	_____
_____	_____	_____	_____
_____	_____	_____	_____
_____	_____	_____	_____

Family #3		Family #4	
Name	Phone #	Name	Phone #
_____	_____	_____	_____
_____	_____	_____	_____
_____	_____	_____	_____
_____	_____	_____	_____
_____	_____	_____	_____
_____	_____	_____	_____

Appendix Three

Suggested Study Group Meeting Format
Introductory Meeting

Note to Facilitator:

— Have copies of the *Introductory Meeting* available for those who do not have a book.

— Have an audio cassette player and tapes available to play relaxing music.

— Familiarize yourself with the materials that are being covered during this meeting.

6:50 [Prior to start of meeting.]

[Play relaxing music. This will help relieve the tension of the day and allow participants to focus on the quiet, comforting presence of God.]

[Distribute copies of the *Introductory Meeting* to those who do not have a book.]

[Reward promptness by starting the meeting on time.]

Opening

7:00 [Allow 20 minutes for *Opening*.]

Facilitator Narrative:

"Welcome to the ***When I Grow Up...I Want To Be An Adult*** study group. My name is _____, and I am your facilitator."

"As we begin our time together, please join me for a moment of silence, followed by the ***Prayer for Serenity***."

Prayer for Serenity

God grant me the serenity to accept the things I cannot change,
the courage to change the things I can,
and the wisdom to know the difference.
Living one day at a time, enjoying one moment at a time;
accepting hardship as a pathway to peace;
taking, as Jesus did, this sinful world as it is,
not as I would have it;
trusting that you will make all things right
if I surrender to your will;
so that I may be reasonably happy in this life
and supremely happy with you forever in the next. Amen

Facilitator Narrative:

"Please introduce yourself by giving your first name only. This respects the anonymity of those who are present. You are not required to disclose your identity."

"Each week at this time I will collect monetary contributions to cover miscellaneous meeting expenses. Next week, we will determine through group consensus how these funds will be distributed (room rental, refreshments, etc.). Announcements can also be made at this time."

"I welcome each of you. Being here is an acknowledgement of your courage to seek support in achieving wholeness in your life. Our backgrounds are many and varied. The common thread is that we were wounded in our development and are seeking healing and wholeness through our Lord Jesus Christ. This study group is one way in which you can gain a better understanding of adult children issues. You can also attend other meetings and read additional materials relating to adult children. This will broaden your understanding of the recovery process and enhance your ability to participate in this program. One of the first lessons in recovery is to know your own limitations and participate in activities that support your recovery."

"During the *Introductory Meeting* and the *Week One Meeting*, you will experience the process used in this support group. You will be asked to make a decision about your personal commitment by the second meeting, which is *Chapter Two*. The full program requires ten weeks of work, study and reflection."

"As you spend time with the group and share your experience, strength and hope with other members, you will find new relationships opening up to you. The quality of these relationships may be unlike any other you have experienced."

"The principle purpose of this support group is to facilitate healing and recovery. You will be asked to do some unfamiliar things, such as trusting others, practicing healthy dependence and interdependence, listening carefully and sharing your feelings. You will have the opportunity to experience what life within a healthy family can be."

Overview of the Program

7:20 [Allow 20 minutes for *Overview*.]

Facilitator Narrative:

"We will take turns reading the overview, one paragraph at a time. Tonight we will read excerpts from the *Invitation to Christ-Centered Recovery* and *How to Benefit Most from This Book*. Feel free to discuss the material either at the end of a paragraph or when the reading is complete."

" Will the person on my left please begin."

Today, many adult Christians who were raised in dysfunctional families suffer from chronic emotional pain brought on by years of parental torment and abuse. To some, the pain is undeniable because the abuse is so great. Others may pretend the pain is insignificant by masking their true feelings.

The purpose of this book is to introduce material which demonstrates the transforming power of Christ-centered recovery. It describes a step-by-step approach to discovering how we can share all of who we are—even the self-defeating thoughts and feelings we hid from ourselves and others. Through sharing honestly and openly with trusted friends, we begin to experience Christ's unconditional love for us. We discover that being loved and cared for by those around us can help to transform our lives. We see that change is possible and is a life-long process that involves focusing on God, ourselves and others.

This book is designed for use by individuals as well as groups. However the material is utilized, there are some basic guidelines to follow. First, read the entire chapter before attempting to answer the questions at the end of the chapter. This provides an overall scope of the material being presented. The *Individual* and *Group Exercises* are important and help make the information in each chapter relevant.

Become familiar with the *Recovery Tool* at the end of each chapter and incorporate it into your ongoing work. Before using the tools, seriously consider creating a personal recovery journal. This is an effective way of recording your progress throughout the program. The journal can be a spiral-bound notebook, a three-ring binder with paper and dividers for each chapter, or a bound book with blank pages. The *Recovery Tool* at the end of the first chapter gives more details about a personal recovery journal.

Pace yourself through each chapter and allow sufficient time to complete the related questions. This may take a day or longer. Be patient with yourself; allow ample time to digest the content of each chapter and reflect on its meaning. Lack of patience can seriously impair your effectiveness.

The appendixes give complete guidelines for using this material in groups. Each meeting lasts two hours, starting and ending promptly. Experience in various meetings shows that trust develops most quickly in small "family groups" with a maximum of seven people. For example, if 24 people participate in a group, divide into four family groups with six members each. The family groups gather to complete the writing exercise and to share together for one hour. The final portion of the meeting is devoted to sharing in one, all-inclusive group.

When participants surrender to guidance from the Holy Spirit, problems can be handled in a constructive and respectful manner. As adult children, we are inclined to be caretakers, enablers and people-pleasers as indicated by our inability to confront inappropriate, hurtful, or self-destructive behavior. In keeping with the need for a safe environment, excessive confrontation is not recommended. However, straightforward feedback is critically important, with communication being limited to each one's personal experience in a given situation.

Wherever possible, share your insights with someone you trust. Seek a special relationship with at least one person in recovery—a fellow pilgrim who is trustworthy and committed to Christ-centered recovery. If you feel you need professional help, refer to *Seeking Help* in *Appendix One*. Intimate and confidential communication with another person can work miracles. Be aware that your listener is not there to give advice or to counsel you, unless trained and licensed to do so.

You may also wish to develop relationships with other participants in your support group. They can become a part of your extended family and a vital lifeline to your ongoing recovery in Christ.

There is no right or wrong way to use the material in this book. No one is grading you. Individuals experience the same material and the same group differently. People grow and change at their own rate according to their own needs.

Writing Exercise

7:40 [Allow 15 minutes for *Writing Exercise*.]

Facilitator Narrative:

"The next 15 minutes will be devoted to the *Writing Exercise*."

"Research involving chemically dependent or emotionally repressed individuals and their families has determined that they share certain negative behaviors. These behaviors reveal an underlying structure of disorder within the family. Although the general popu- lation demonstrates many of these same behaviors, individuals from dysfunctional fami-lies tend to exhibit these behaviors in the extreme. This exercise is intended to help you identify whether or not there are areas of your life in which dysfunctional beavior is evident."

"When I have completed reading the *Common Symptoms of Adult Children*, please answer the questions on page 171."

Common Symptoms of Adult Children

— We are incapable of building and maintaining enduring, meaningful and intimate relationships with God, ourselves, or others.

— We find it difficult to trust ourselves or others in a deepening fashion; thus, it is hard for us to live by faith.

— We do not possess the skills or vocabulary necessary for the healthy communication of feelings, preferences, ideas, or needs.

— We do not know how to manage the inevitable stresses of life; we cannot easily play, relax, or rest.

— We do not possess the skills necessary to understand God's will in our lives.

— We are resistant to change.

— We are rigid and inflexible in our thoughts and actions.

— We lack the ability to grow spiritually and emotionally.

— We do not know how or where to seek help or to offer help to others.

— We do not know how to handle adult responsibilities and relationships.

— We often feel that we do not belong anywhere.

— We have difficulty developing healthy beliefs, morals and values.

— We have a strong need to be in control.

— We have difficulty following projects from beginning to end.

— We feel guilty when we stand up for ourselves.

— We give in to others instead of taking care of ourselves.

● Choose two of the symptoms that describe you and write about how these symptoms currently affect your life. _____

_____

_____

_____

_____

● What changes would you like to see in your life as a result of participating in this recovery program? _____

_____

_____

_____

_____

Family Group Sharing

7:55 [Separate into groups of five to seven and allow 30 minutes for *Family Group Sharing*.]

Facilitator Narrative:

"The next 30 minutes is devoted to *Family Group Sharing*."

"We will form small groups of five to seven people for this portion of the meeting. These groups are called family groups. An important part of this program is being able to feel safe within the family group. A small group atmosphere encourages healthy, nurturing, family-type communication between participants. It provides a safe atmosphere where trust can be learned and serves as an arena for quality sharing. Permanent family groups will be formed for the second meeting which is *Chapter Two*."

"Sharing your written work within each group will last 30 minutes. Focus on your writing and allow everyone to share, answering one question at a time."

"Please divide the sharing time equally among family group members. Limit individual sharing to the responses to the *Writing Exercise*. Further contributions to sharing can take place if time allows."

"Please refrain from 'crosstalk.' Accept, without comment, what others say because it is true for them. Crosstalk occurs when two or more people have a dialogue which excludes the other participants and becomes advice giving. Take responsibility for your own feelings, thoughts and actions instead of giving advice to others."

"Focus your sharing on your own experiences relative to the *Writing Exercise*. This allows you to convey valuable insights and share your experience, strength and hope with others."

"Please form small groups of five to seven people and begin sharing."

Meeting Guidelines

8:25 [Rejoin into one large group and allow 20 minutes to read and discuss *Meeting Guidelines*.]

Facilitator Narrative:

"Please join into one large group."

"We will take turns reading the *Principles for Christ-Centered Study Groups* and the *Ground Rules for Christ-Centered Study Groups*, one statement at a time. Feel free to discuss the material either at the end of a statement or when the reading is complete."

" Will the person on my left please begin."

Principles for Christ-Centered Study Groups

There are five basic principles with biblical references which are an important part of Christ-centered recovery. These principles should be followed each time the group meets.

Provide a non-threatening system of mutual accountability.

"Is any one of you in trouble? He should pray. Is any one happy? Let him sing songs of praise. Is any one of you sick? He should call the elders of the church to pray over him and anoint him with oil in the name of the Lord. And the prayer offered in faith will make the sick person well; the Lord will raise him up. If he has sinned, he will be forgiven. Therefore confess your sins to each other and pray for each other so that you may be healed. The prayer of a righteous man is powerful and effective."
JAMES 5:13-16 (NIV)

An example of mutual accountability is one member calling another member each day for prayer and support in abstaining from a harmful habit. This is especially helpful during the first phase of withdrawal from self-defeating habits, such as abusive use of chemicals, food, sex, gambling, or work. The person being supported can give and receive strength and courage by reporting the results to the whole group.

Minister to specific areas of need with directed prayer each time the group meets.

"Pray continually; give thanks in all circumstances, for this is God's will for you in Christ Jesus."
1 THESSALONIANS 5:17 (NIV)

In order to illustrate this crucial principle, it is necessary to understand how prone we are to denial and self-deception. By openly sharing our thoughts and feelings with trusted and supportive friends, we can receive help clarifying our specific needs and focusing prayer on certain problem areas in our lives.

Minister to each person in the group according to their needs.

"If one part suffers, every part suffers with it; if one part is honored, every part rejoices with it. Now you are the body of Christ, and each one of you is a part of it." 1 CORINTHIANS 12:26-27 (NIV)

Participation in support groups can help us free ourselves from the past, live honestly in the present and have realistic expectations, plans and goals for the future. If we tend to project the blame for our problems on past circumstances or future fears—"I wouldn't be overeating if my parents had shown me more love" or "I can't be expected to quit smoking with a big deadline coming up"—we can learn, through group interaction, to focus on *today*. By working toward a common goal of healing and wholeness, group members can learn to manage their lives in a positive, healthy manner—one day at a time.

Encourage one another to progress from a state of physical, emotional and spiritual sickness to wholeness of life.

"...consider how we may spur one another on toward love and good deeds." HEBREWS 10:24 (NIV)

Many times we are like a mule who stubbornly sits down when in the middle of plowing a fresh row. The farmer has to encourage and provoke the mule to finish the task at hand. We need others to support us as we move from a comfortable place toward a less comfortable place, where we can change our lives and impact our future.

Aid one another in applying biblical truths to personal and relationship needs.

"Jesus said, 'If you hold to my teaching, you are really my disciples. Then you will know the truth, and the truth will set you free.'" JOHN 8:31-32 (NIV)

Confession is one way the members of a support group might apply this principle to their lives. When we confess our sins to Christ, we receive cleansing and forgiveness. When group members openly share their faults with one another, honesty, trust and healing occur. When sharing in this way, we focus on how the truth is currently working in our lives. Remember, it is inappropriate to quote Scripture or engage in theological discussions while sharing.

Ground Rules for Christ-Centered Study Groups

Experience has shown that the following ground rules aid Christ-centered recovery groups in promoting integrity, maintaining consistency and assuring a healthy supportive process.

Come prepared to each meeting.

Read the chapter material and review the *Group Exercise*.

Pray for guidance and the willingness to be open and honest when sharing your past and present life experiences with other group members.

Complete the *Individual Exercise*.

Record in your personal recovery journal any personal insights gained or changes desired as a result of your reading.

Communicate with at least one other support group participant between meetings.

Maintain confidentiality.

Keep whatever is shared within the confines of the group to provide an atmosphere of safety and openness.

Pray for one another. Private prayers can be effective and powerful.

Refrain from gossip.

Share your own needs, and do not talk about someone who is not present.

Encourage comfort and support by sharing from personal experience, strength and hope.

Support others. Do not give advice or try to rescue them. When we come together as a group, we can comfort each other, as we have been comforted by God. This type of interaction is one reason that the group process works so well. If we are struggling with a problem, we often find at least one other person who has worked through a similar struggle. An individual who is recovering from the effects of self-defeating behavior (e.g., addiction to chemicals, food, sex, or unhealthy relationships) is often the one best equipped to minister to those striving to overcome a similar problem. When we meet with others for whom God's promise of comfort has become a reality, we begin to see light at the end of the tunnel.

Make a point of ministering love in an appropriate manner.

Respect others' needs by asking what they would feel comfortable receiving. Many people do not know how to ask for affection or to recognize they are loved simply by a friendly touch or warm hug. It is important to use discretion and express affection in a manner appropriate to the individual.

Refrain from criticizing or defending other members.

Hold others accountable for their behavior in a loving manner if they ask you to do so. Otherwise, recognize that we are all accountable to Christ. The emphasis in Christ-centered study groups is to attend the meetings for our own needs and to comfort others; not to choose sides, come to the defense of others, or to criticize them.

Limit our own talking and allow others to share.

Allow everyone in the group to have an equal opportunity to share. Talk about your own experience, strength and hope without giving a full-length autobiography. Share an event or a feeling rather than your ideology, theology, intentions, or opinions. Take turns talking, and do not interrupt each other.

Recognize that the Holy Spirit is in charge.

Realize that the leader is simply facilitating the group. Pray for guidance and discretion, and ask the Holy Spirit to be present within each of you.

Refrain from crosstalk.

Accept, without comment, what others say because it is true for them. Take responsibility for your own feelings, thoughts and actions instead of giving advice to others. "Crosstalk" occurs when two or more people have a dialogue which excludes the other participants and becomes advice giving.

Review

8:45 [Allow 10 minutes for *Review*.]

Facilitator Narrative:

"The principle commitment required to successfully complete this work is a willingness to engage in the process one day at a time, one meeting at a time. It is also vital to trust God to take care of the outcome."

"The weekly meetings are similar to what you experienced in this meeting. Fifteen minutes is allocated to the *Writing Exercise*, followed by one hour of *Family Group Sharing* and *Family Group Prayer Requests*. There will be time during each meeting for prayer requests within each family group."

"As the facilitator of the meeting, my purpose is to be your trusted servant. I will work the material with you. Understand that I am here, as I believe you are, to share my experience, strength and hope. I will lead only the *Introductory Meeting* and *Week One* meeting. By *Week Two*, which is *Chapter Two*, family groups will have been formed, and each group will be responsible for leading the meeting on a rotating basis. Rather than being assigned to a specific family group, I will participate with the group that is leading the meeting."

"Does anyone have any questions relative to the material presented tonight or to this study group?"

Closing

8:55 [Allow 5 minutes for *Closing*.]

Facilitator Narrative:

"If you plan to participate in this group, please purchase a book. Next week we will begin with *Chapter One, Who Am I?* Please read *Chapter One* and complete the *Individual Exercise* prior to the next meeting."

"*Week One* will be open to newcomers. If you wish to invite others to join us, please contact them prior to next week's meeting. The meeting two weeks from now, *Chapter Two*, will be closed to new members."

"What you hear at this meeting is confidential; leave it at this meeting; it is not for public disclosure or gossip. Please respect the privacy of those who shared tonight."

"Will all who care to, join me in the closing prayer. My selection for tonight's prayer is *The Lord's Prayer*."

9:00 [Adjourn.]

Suggested Study Group Meeting Format
Week One Meeting Format

Note to Facilitator:

— Have 3x5 cards available for individuals who plan to continue participating in the program. These cards will be used to form family groups and create a roster prior to the next meeting.

— Have an audio cassette player and tapes available to play relaxing music.

— Familiarize yourself with the materials that are being covered during this meeting.

— Assign individuals to read the *Principles for Christ-Centered Study Groups* and *Ground Rules for Christ-Centered Study Groups*.

— Review the meeting format and assign an individual to announce the times for writing, sharing, praying, etc.

6:50 [Prior to start of meeting.]

[Play relaxing music. This will help relieve the tension of the day and allow participants to focus on the quiet, comforting presence of God.]

[Reward promptness by starting the meeting on time.]

Opening

7:00 [Allow 10 minutes for *Opening*.]

Facilitator Narrative:
"Good evening. My name is _____. I am your facilitator, and I will be your leader for this evening. Next week we will rotate leadership by family group, beginning with Family Group #1."

"We will now open the meeting with a moment of silence, followed by the *Prayer for Serenity*."

Prayer for Serenity

God grant me the serenity to
accept the things I cannot change,
the courage to change the things I can,
and the wisdom to know the difference.
Living one day at a time,
enjoying one moment at a time;
accepting hardship as a pathway to peace;
taking, as Jesus did,
this sinful world as it is,

> *not as I would have it;*
> *trusting that you will make all things right*
> *if I surrender to your will;*
> *so that I may be reasonably happy in this life*
> *and supremely happy with you forever in the next.*
> *Amen.*

Facilitator Narrative:

"We are self-supporting through our own monetary contributions. We will take a few moments now to determine through group consensus how the funds collected will be distributed (literature, room rental, refreshments, etc.). At the final meeting we will discuss what will be done with any excess funds. Does anyone have any suggestions?"

"Please make your contributions at this time to avoid interrupting the meeting."

"Are there any announcements?"

"I have asked _____ to read the *Principles for Christ-Centered Study Groups.*"

Principles for Christ-Centered Study Groups

As participants in this study group, we agree to abide by these principles:

— Provide a non-threatening system of mutual accountability.

— Minister to specific areas of need with directed prayer each time the group meets.

— Minister to each person in the group according to their needs.

— Encourage one another to progress from a state of physical, emotional and spiritual sickness to wholeness of life.

— Aid one another in applying biblical truths to personal and relationship needs.

Facilitator Narrative:

"I have asked _____ to read the *Ground Rules for Christ-Centered Study Groups.*"

Ground Rules for Christ-Centered Study Groups

As participants in this study group, we also agree to abide by these ground rules.

— Come prepared to each meeting.

— Maintain confidentiality.

— Refrain from gossip.

— Encourage comfort and support by sharing our own personal experience, strength and hope.

— Make a point of ministering love in an appropriate manner.

— Refrain from criticizing or defending other members.

— Limit our own talking and allow others to share.

— Recognize that the Holy Spirit is in charge.

— Refrain from crosstalk.

Writing Exercise

7:10 [Allow 15 minutes for *Writing Exercise*.]

Facilitator Narrative:

"The next 15 minutes will be spent completing the *Group Exercise* for *Chapter One* on page 18, followed by 45 minutes of *Family Group Sharing* and 15 minutes of prayer. There will be a 10 minute break at 8:25, after which we will join together for large group sharing."

Family Group Sharing

7:25 [Allow 45 minutes for *Family Group Sharing*.]

Facilitator Narrative:

"The next 45 minutes will be devoted to *Family Group Sharing*."

"When sharing, focus on your writing first and allow time for everyone to share, answering one question at a time. Refrain from crosstalk, where two people enter into a dialogue that excludes other group members."

"After everyone has shared what was written, open discussion can take place on matters related to this week's chapter and other similar topics."

"The last question in the *Writing Exercise* pertains to your prayer request. Please share your response to this question during *Family Group Prayer Requests*."

"Your sharing is most valuable when you limit your comments to your own personal experience. Refrain from engaging in small talk that can distract others from the focus of the meeting. It is not necessary for everyone to share."

"Please form small groups of five to seven people and begin sharing."

Family Group Prayer Requests

8:10 [Allow 15 minutes for *Family Group Prayer Requests*.]

Facilitator Narrative:

"The next 15 minutes will be devoted to *Family Group Prayer Requests*."

"Refer to your prayer request for yourself or others in the *Group Exercise*."

"We can make progress in our recovery and achieve the healing we desire with the assistance of God and the encouragement of those around us. By requesting and offering prayer support, we have an opportunity to be honest about our personal needs and concerns. Remember that it is inappropriate to give advice or offer solutions when responding to the prayer requests of other group members."

"At 8:25, we will take a 10 minute break, then form into the large group."

Meeting Break

8:25 [Allow 10 minutes for *Meeting Break* and forming the large group.]

Large Group Sharing

8:35 [Allow 20 minutes for *Large Group Sharing*.]

Facilitator Narrative:

"The next 20 minutes will be devoted to *Large Group Sharing*."

"Please introduce yourself prior to sharing. Limit your sharing to 3 minutes so that everyone will have an opportunity to share. It is important to share our pleasant experiences as well as our unpleasant ones."

"Does anyone have a recovery experience from the material, an insight from journaling, or comments on the family group interaction from last week?"

Closing

8:55 [Allow 5 minutes for *Closing*.]

Facilitator Narrative:

"At this time I am going to distribute 3x5 cards. If you plan to participate in this group, please fill out a card with your first name, last initial and telephone number. Family groups are selected at random by dividing the cards into groups. This has been proven to be a safe and non-judgmental appoach to family group selection. It is a big step toward letting go and trusting in the recovery process."

"It is advisable that you are not in a group with a person with whom you are in a relationship. Please note special requests on your card."

"The meeting will be closed to newcomers next week."

"Next week, I will distribute a *Family Group Roster* with family assignments and telephone numbers. Please sit with your assigned family at the beginning of the meeting."

"Family group #1 will lead the meeting next week."

"Reminder! What you hear at this meeting is confidential. Leave it at this meeting. It is not for public disclosure or gossip. Please respect the privacy of those who shared with us tonight. This is an essential part of the recovery process and violating it can cause damage beyond repair."

"Will everyone please help clean and rearrange the room."

"Will all who care to, join me in the closing prayer. My selection for tonight's prayer is _____."

[Prayer suggestions: *The Lord's Prayer*, the *Prayer for Serenity*, or a prayer of your choosing.]

9:00 [Adjourn.]

Suggested Study Group Meeting Format
Week Two Meeting Format

Note to Facilitator:
— Have copies of the *Family Group Roster* available.
— Have an audio cassette player and tapes available to play relaxing music.
— Familiarize yourself with the materials that are being covered during this meeting.

Note to Family Group Leader:
— Set up the room and arrange the chairs to accommodate the small groups.
— Assign group members to read the *Principles for Christ-Centered Study Groups* and *Ground Rules for Christ-Centered Study Groups*.
— Review the meeting format and assign a member to announce the times for writing, sharing, praying, etc.

6:50 [Prior to start of meeting.]

[Play relaxing music. This will help relieve the tension of the day and allow participants to focus on the quiet, comforting presence of God.]

[Reward promptness by starting the meeting on time.]

Opening

7:00 [Allow 10 minutes for *Opening*.]

Facilitator Narrative:

"Before beginning the meeting, I am going to distribute the *Family Group Roster*. Will everyone please sit with their assigned group. These are your family groups for the duration of the study group. Each week, please join with your family group at 7:00."

"Family group #1 is the leader for this meeting. Within your group, please assign a member to lead the meeting."

Family Group Leader Narrative:

"Good evening. My name is _____. I represent family group #1, and we are the leaders for this evening."

"We will now open the meeting with a moment of silence, followed by the *Prayer for Serenity*."

Prayer for Serenity

God grant me the serenity
to accept the things I cannot change,
the courage to change the things I can,
and the wisdom to know the difference.
Living one day at a time,
enjoying one moment at a time;
accepting hardship as a pathway to peace;
taking, as Jesus did,
this sinful world as it is,
not as I would have it;
trusting that you will make all things right
if I surrender to your will;
so that I may be reasonably happy in this life
and supremely happy with you forever in the next.
Amen.

Family Group Leader Narrative:
"We are self-supporting through our own monetary contributions. Please make your contributions at this time to avoid interrupting the meeting."
"Are there any announcements?"
"I have asked _____ to read the *Principles for Christ-Centered Study Groups*."

Principles for Christ-Centered Study Groups

As participants in this study group, we agree to abide by these principles:

— Provide a non-threatening system of mutual accountability.

— Minister to specific areas of need with directed prayer each time the group meets.

— Minister to each person in the group according to their needs.

— Encourage one another to progress from a state of physical, emotional and spiritual sickness to wholeness of life.

— Aid one another in applying biblical truths to personal and relationship needs.

Family Group Leader Narrative:
"I have asked _____ to read the *Ground Rules for Christ-Centered Study Groups*."

Ground Rules for Christ-Centered Study Groups

As participants in this study group, we also agree to abide by these ground rules:

— Come prepared to each meeting.

- Maintain confidentiality.
- Refrain from gossip.
- Encourage comfort and support by sharing from personal experience, strength and hope.
- Make a point of ministering love in an appropriate manner.
- Refrain from criticizing or defending other members.
- Limit our own talking and allow others to share.
- Recognize that the Holy Spirit is in charge.
- Refrain from crosstalk.

Writing Exercise

7:10 [Allow 15 minutes for *Writing Exercise*.]

> **Family Group Leader Narrative:**
> "The next 15 minutes will be spent completing the *Group Exercise* for *Chapter Two* on page 30, followed by 45 minutes of *Family Group Sharing* and 15 minutes of prayer. There will be a 10 minute break at 8:25, after which we will join together for *Large Group Sharing*."
> "If members of your family group are absent, please make arrangements to contact them in order to encourage and support their attendance."

Family Group Sharing

7:25 [Allow 45 minutes for *Family Group Sharing*.]

> **Family Group Leader Narrative:**
> "The next 45 minutes will be devoted to *Family Group Sharing*. As part of your sharing, please introduce yourself and give a brief history of your background."
> "When sharing your writing, allow time for everyone to share, answering one question at a time. Refrain from crosstalk, where two people enter into a dialogue that excludes other group members and becomes advice giving. Take responsibility for your own feelings, thoughts and actions instead of giving advice to others."
> "After everyone has shared what was written, open discussion can take place on matters related to this week's chapter and other similar topics."
> "The last question in the *Writing Exercise* pertains to your prayer request. Please share your response to this question during *Family Group Prayer Requests*."
> "Your sharing is most valuable when you limit your comments to your own personal experience. Refrain from engaging in small talk that can distract others from the focus of the meeting. It is not necessary for everyone to share."

Family Group Prayer Requests

8:10 [Allow 15 minutes for *Family Group Prayer Requests*.]

Facilitator Group Leader Narrative:

"The next 15 minutes will be devoted to *Family Group Prayer Requests*."

"Refer to your prayer request for yourself or others in the *Group Exercise*."

"We can make progress in our recovery and achieve the healing we desire with the assistance of God and the encouragement of those around us. By requesting and offering prayer support, we have an opportunity to be honest about our personal needs and concerns. Remember that it is inappropriate to give advice or offer solutions when responding to the prayer requests of other group members."

"At 8:25, we will take a 10 minute break, then form into the large group."

Meeting Break

8:25 [Allow 10 minutes for *Meeting Break*.]

Large Group Sharing

8:35 [Allow 20 minutes for *Large Group Sharing*.]

FamilyGroup Leader Narrative:

"The next 20 minutes will be devoted to *Large Group Sharing*."

"Please introduce yourself prior to sharing. Limit your sharing to 3 minutes so that everyone will have an opportunity to share. It is important to share our pleasant experiences as well as our unpleasant ones."

"Does anyone have an answered prayer from a prayer request, a recovery experience from the material, an insight from journaling, or comments on the family group interaction last week?"

Closing

8:55 [Allow 5 minutes for *Closing*.]

Family Group Leader Narrative:

"Our time for sharing is over. All of you are encouraged to meet at another time during the week to process writing and to deepen family group bonding and trust. An alternative to meeting in person is being in contact by telephone."

"Family Group #2 will lead the meeting next week."

"Reminder! What you hear at this meeting is confidential. Leave it at this meeting. It is not for public disclosure or gossip. Please respect the privacy of those who shared with us tonight. This is an essential part of the recovery process, and violating it can cause damage beyond repair."

"Will everyone please help clean and rearrange the room."

"Will all who care to, join me in the closing prayer. My selection for tonight's prayer is _____."

[Prayer suggestions: *The Lord's Prayer*, the *Prayer for Serenity,* or a prayer of your choosing.]

9:00 [Adjourn.]

Suggested Study Group Meeting Format
Week Three to Week Ten Meeting Format

Note to Facilitator:

— Have an audio cassette player and tapes available to play relaxing music.

— Familiarize yourself with the materials that are being covered during this meeting.

Note to Family Group Leader:

— Set up the room and arrange the chairs to accommodate the small groups.

— Assign group members to read the *Principles for Christ-Centered Study Groups* and *Ground Rules for Christ-Centered Study Groups*.

— Review the meeting format and assign a member to announce the times for writing, sharing, praying, etc.

6:50 [Prior to start of meeting.]

[Play relaxing music. This will help relieve the tension of the day and allow participants to focus on the quiet, comforting presence of God.]

[Reward promptness by starting the meeting on time.]

Opening

7:00 [Allow 10 minutes for *Opening*.]

Family Group Leader Narrative:
"Good evening. My name is _____. I represent family group # ___, and we are the leaders for this evening."
"Will all who care to, please join me in the *Prayer for Serenity*."

Prayer for Serenity

God grant me the serenity to accept the things I cannot change,
the courage to change the things I can,
and the wisdom to know the difference.
Living one day at a time, enjoying one moment at a time;
accepting hardship as a pathway to peace;
taking, as Jesus did, this sinful world as it is,
not as I would have it;
trusting that you will make all things right
if I surrender to your will;
so that I may be reasonably happy in this life
and supremely happy with you forever in the next. Amen.

Principles for Christ-Centered Study Groups

As participants in this study group, we agree to abide by these principles:

— Provide a non-threatening system of mutual accountability.

— Minister to specific areas of need with directed prayer each time the group meets.

— Minister to each person in the group according to their needs.

— Encourage one another to progress from a state of physical, emotional and spiritual sickness to wholeness of life.

— Aid one another in applying biblical truths to personal and relationship needs.

Ground Rules for Christ-Centered Study Groups

As participants in this study group, we also agree to abide by these ground rules:

— Come prepared to each meeting.

— Maintain confidentiality.

— Refrain from gossip.

— Encourage comfort and support by sharing from personal experience, strength and hope.

— Make a point of ministering love in an appropriate manner.

— Refrain from criticizing or defending other members.

— Limit our own talking and allow others to share.

— Recognize that the Holy Spirit is in charge.

— Refrain from crosstalk.

Writing Exercise

7:10 [Allow 15 minutes for *Writing Exercise*.]

Family Group Leader Narrative:

"The next 15 minutes will be spent completing the *Group Exercise* for *Chapter* ___ on page ___, followed by 45 minutes of *Family Group Sharing* and 15 minutes of prayer. There will be a 10 minute break at 8:25, after which we will join together for *Large Group Sharing*."

"If members of your family group are absent, please make arrangements to contact them in order to encourage and support their attendance."

Family Group Sharing

7:25 [Allow 45 minutes for *Family Group Sharing*.]

Family Group Leader Narrative:

"The next 45 minutes will be devoted to *Family Group Sharing*. As part of your sharing, please introduce yourself and give a brief history of your background."

"When sharing your writing, allow time for everyone to share, answering one question at a time. Refrain from crosstalk, where two people enter into a dialogue that excludes other group members and becomes advice giving. Take responsibility for your own feelings, thoughts and actions instead of giving advice to others."

"After everyone has shared what was written, open discussion can take place on matters related to this week's chapter and other similar topics."

"The last question in the *Writing Exercise* pertains to your prayer request. Please share your response to this question during *Family Group Prayer Requests*."

"Your sharing is most valuable when you limit your comments to your own personal experience. Refrain from engaging in small talk that can distract others from the focus of the meeting. It is not necessary for everyone to share."

Family Group Prayer Requests

8:10 [Allow 15 minutes for *Family Group Prayer Requests*.]

Family Group Leader Narrative:

"The next 15 minutes will be devoted to *Family Group Prayer Requests*."

"Refer to your prayer request for yourself or others in the *Group Exercise*."

"We can make progress in our recovery and achieve the healing we desire with the assistance of God and the encouragement of those around us. By requesting and offering prayer support, we have an opportunity to be honest about our personal needs and concerns. Remember that it is inappropriate to give advice or offer solutions when responding to the prayer requests of other group members."

"At 8:25 we will take a 10 minute break, then form into the large group."

Meeting Break

8:25 [Allow 10 minutes for *Meeting Break* and forming the large group.]

Large Group Sharing

Family Group Leader Narrative:
"The next 20 minutes will be devoted to *Large Group Sharing*."
"Please introduce yourself prior to sharing. Limit your sharing to 3 minutes so that everyone will have an opportunity to share."
"Does someone have an answered prayer from a prayer request, a recovery experience from the material, an insight from journaling, or results from family group interaction during the previous week? It is important to share our pleasant experiences as well as our unpleasant ones."

8:35 [Allow 20 minutes for *Large Group Sharing*.]

Closing

8:55 [Allow 5 minutes for *Closing*.]

Family Group Leader Narrative:
"Our time for sharing is over. All of you are encouraged to meet at another time during the week to process writing and to deepen family group bonding and trust. An alternative to meeting in person is being in contact by telephone."
"Family group #___ will lead the meeting next week."
"Reminder! What you hear at this meeting is confidential. Leave it at this meeting. It is not for public disclosure or gossip. Please respect the privacy of those who shared with us tonight. This is an essential part of the recovery process, and violating it can cause damage beyond repair."
"Will everyone please help clean and rearrange the room."
"Will all who care to, join me in the closing prayer. My selection for tonight's prayer is _____."

[Prayer suggestions: *The Lord's Prayer*, the *Prayer for Serenity*, or a prayer of your choosing.]

9:00 [Adjourn.]

Appendix Four

The Twelve Steps and Related Scripture

Step One

We admitted we were powerless over our separation from God—that our lives had become unmanageable

> *I know nothing good lives in me, that is, in my sinful nature. For I have the desire to do what is good, but I cannot carry it out.* ROMANS 7:18 (NIV).

Step Two

Came to believe that a power greater than ourselves could restore us to sanity.

> *For it is God who works in you to will and to act according to his good purpose.* PHILIPPIANS 2:13 (NIV).

Step Three

Made a decision to turn our will and our lives over to the care of God *as we understood Him.*

> *Therefore, I urge you, brothers, in view of God's mercy, to offer your bodies as living sacrifices, holy and pleasing to God—which is your spiritual worship.* ROMANS 12:1 (NIV).

Step Four

Made a searching and fearless moral inventory of ourselves.

> *Let us examine our ways and test them, and let us return to the Lord.* LAMENTATIONS 3:40 (NIV).

Step Five

Admitted to God, to ourselves, and to another human being the exact nature of our wrongs.

> *Therefore confess your sins to each other and pray for each other so that you may be healed.* JAMES 5:16A (NIV).

Step Six

Were entirely ready to have God remove all these defects of character.

> *Humble yourselves before the Lord, and he will lift you up.* JAMES 4:10 (NIV).

Step Seven

Humbly asked Him to remove our shortcomings.

> *If we confess our sins, he is faithful and just and will forgive us our sins and purify us form all unrighteousness.* 1 JOHN 1:9 (NIV).

Step Eight

Made a list of all persons we had harmed and became willing to make amends to them all.

> *Do unto others as you would have them do to you.* LUKE 6:31 (NIV).

Step Nine

Made direct amends to such people wherever possible, except when to do so would injure them or others.

> *Therefore, if you are offering your gift at the altar and there remember that your brother has something against you, leave your gift there in front of the altar. First go and be reconciled to your brother; then come and offer your gift.* MATTHEW 5:23-24 (NIV).

Step Ten

Continued to take personal inventory and, when we were wrong, promptly admitted it.

> *So, if you think you are standing firm, be careful that you don't fall.* 1 CORINTHIANS 10:12 (NIV).

Step Eleven

Sought through prayer and meditation to improve our conscious contact with God *as we understood Him*, praying only for knowledge of His will for us and the power to carry that out.

> *Let the word of Christ dwell in you richly.* COLOSSIANS 3:16A (NIV).

Step Twelve

Having had a spiritual awakening as the result of these steps, we tried to carry this message to others, and to practice these principles in all our affairs.

> *"Brothers, if someone is caught in a sin, you who are spiritual should restore him gently. But watch yourself, or you also may be tempted.* GALATIANS 6:1 (NIV).

Self-Help Resources
Christian Groups

Alcoholics for Christ
1316 N. Campbell Road
Royal Oak, Michigan 48067
(800) 441-7877

Alcoholics Victorious
National Headquarters
P.O. Box 10364
Portland, Oregon 97210
(503) 245-9629

Christian Alcoholics
Rehabilitation Association
F O A Road
Pocahontas, Mississippi 39072

Dunklin Memorial Camp
3342 S.W. Hosannah Lane
Okeechobee, Florida 34974
(407) 597-2841

Ephesians 5:18 Life Ministries
966 Hungerford Drive, Suite 16B
Rockville, Maryland 20850

Faith Farms
9538 Highway 441
Boynton Beach, Florida 33436

Free Indeed
P.O. Box 630
Idaho Springs, Colorado 80452

Fresh Start
P.O. Box 1734
Orlando, Florida 32802

House of Hope
P.O. Box 560484
Orlando, Florida 32856

Liberty Lodge
4050 Coquina Avenue
Titusville, Florida 32780

Liontamers
2801 North Brea Boulevard
Fullerton, California 92635-2799
(714) 529-5544

Lost and Found
9189 South Turkey Creek Road
Morrison, Colorado 80465

National Association for Christian Recovery
P.O. Box 11095
Whittier, California 90603

The Net Institute
1454 E. Semoran Avenue
Casselberry, Florida 32707
(407) 671-0900

New Hope Fellowship Groups
Heritage Church
Ft. Mill, South Carolina 29715

New Life Treatment Center
P.O. Box 38
Woodstock, Minnesota 56186

Open Homes Ministries
P.O. Box 679022
Orlando, Florida 32867
(407) 671-0900

Pressing Onward Support Groups
(New England and Canada)
His Mansion
P.O. Box 40
Hillsboro, New Hampshire 03244-0040

Skyline Wesleyan Church
1345 Skyline Drive
Lemon Grove, California 92045
(619) 460-5000

Secular Groups

Adult Children of Alcoholics
Central Service Board
P.O. Box 3216
Torrance, California 90505
(213) 534-1815

Al-Anon/Alateen
Family Group Headquarters, Inc.
Madison Square Station
New York, New York 10010
(212) 683-1771

Alcoholics Anonymous
World Services, Inc.
468 Park Avenue South
New York, New York 10016
(212) 686-1100

Co-Dependents Anonymous
P.O. Box5508
Glendale, Arizona 85312
(602) 979-1751

Debtors Anonymous
P.O. Box 20322
New York, New York 10025-9992

Substance Abusers Victorious
One Cascade Plaza
Akron, Ohio 44308

Youth Challenge
P.O. Box 999
Wildwood, Florida 32785

Emotions Anonymous
P.O. Box 4245
St. Paul, Minnesota 55104

Gamblers Anonymous
P.O. Box 17173
Los Angeles, California 90017

Narcotics Anonymous
World Service Office
16155 Wyandotte Street
Van Nuys, California 91406
(818) 780-3951

National Association for
Children of Alcoholics
31706 Coast Highway, Suite 201
South Laguna, California 92677

Overeaters Anonymous
World Service Office
2190 190th Street
Torrance, California 90504
(213) 320-7941

Sexaholics Anonymous
P.O. Box 300
Simi Valley, California 93062

Suggested Reading

Clemmons, Dr. Bill. **Discovering the Depths.** Nashville, TN: Broadman Press.

Crabb, Larry. **Healing From The Inside/Out.** Colorado Springs, CO: Navigators Press.

Dodson, Dr. James. **Love Must Be Tough.** Waco, TX: Word Publishers.

Drummond, Henry. **The Changed Life.** Titusville, FL: Soul Care Inc.

Dunkin Memorial Camp. **Overcomer's Manual.** Okeechobee, FL: Dunkin Memorial Camp.

Friel, John and Friel, Linda. **Adult Children—The Secrets of Dysfunctional Families.** Deerfield Beach, FL: Health Communications, Inc.

Friends in Recovery. **The Twelve Steps for Christians.** San Diego, CA: Recovery Publications, Inc.

Friends in Recovery. **The Twelve Steps—A Spiritual Journey.** San Diego, CA: Recovery Publications, Inc.

Fromk, Devern. **Life's Ultimate Privilege.** Titusville, FL: Soul Care, Inc.

Hemfelt, Dr. Robert, Minirth; Dr. Frank, and Meier; Dr. Paul. **Love Is A Choice**. Nashville, TN: Thomas Nelson, Inc.

Hill, Sally. **New Clothes from Old Threads**. San Diego, CA: Recovery Publications, Inc.

Jabay, Earl. **The Kingdom Of Self.** Plainfield, NJ: Logos International Publishers

LeSourd, Sandra Simpson. **The Compulsive Woman.** Old Tappan, NJ: Chosen Books.

Linn, Dennis and Matthew. **Healing Life's Hurts.** New York, NY: Paulist Press.

May, Dr. Gerald C. **Addiction and Grace.** New York, NY: HarperCollins Publishers.

McGinnis, Jack and Shlemon, Barbara. **The Truth Will Set You Free**. San Diego, CA: Recovery Publications, Inc.

Rinck, Dr. Margaret. **Can Christians Love Too Much?** Grand Rapids, MI: Zondervan Publishing House.

Sanford, John and Paula. **New Life for Your Adopted Child.** South Plainfield, NJ: Bridge Publishing, Inc.

Sanford, John and Paula. **Restoring the Christian Family.** South Plainfield, NJ: Bridge Publishing, Inc.

Sanford, John and Paula. **Transformation of the Inner Man.** South Plainfield, NJ: Bridge Publishing, Inc.

Order Form

9906	New Clothes from Old Threads	_____	$15.95	_____
9907	The Truth Will Set You Free (Workbook)	_____	$10.95	_____
9007	The Truth Will Set You Free (Book & Video)	_____	$99.95	_____
9902	The 12 Steps for Adult Children	_____	$ 7.95	_____
9901	The 12 Steps—A Way Out	_____	$14.95	_____
9904	The Twelve Steps for Christians	_____	$ 7.95	_____
9903	The Twelve Steps—A Spiritual Journey	_____	$14.95	_____
9905	When I Grow Up . . . I Want To Be An Adult	_____	$12.95	_____
			Subtotal	_____
			*Sales Tax	_____
			**Shipping & Handling	_____
			TOTAL	_____

Visa and **MasterCard** Accepted

_____
Bankcard No.

_____
Expiration Date

_____
Signature

* California residents add applicable sales tax.

COD orders—add $3.75 to shipping cost.

** Shipping and Handling:
   Minimum Charge $3.00
   Orders over $25.00—$5.00
   Orders over $50.00, add 10%
      of Subtotal.

To Order by Phone: (619) 275-1350 or (800) 873-8384
To Order by FAX: (619) 275-5729

Or send this order form and a check or money order (U.S. funds only) for the total to:

Tools for Recovery
1201 Knoxville Street
San Diego, CA 92110-3718

Name: _____

Address:_____

City/State/Zip:_____

Phone: _____